CW00386136

Leah Manning

LEAH MANNING

by
RON BILL
and
STAN NEWENS

LEAH MANNING TRUST
in association with
SQUARE ONE BOOKS LIMITED

LEAH MANNING

© Ron Bill and Stan Newens 1991

All rights reserved.
No part of this publication may be reproduced,
stored in a retrieval system, or transmitted in any form
or by any means, electronic, mechanical,
photocopying, recording or otherwise,
without the prior permission of the Publisher
or the copyright owner.

First published in 1991 by
THE LEAH MANNING TRUST, HARLOW, ESSEX
In association with
SQUARE ONE BOOKS LTD, BRENTWOOD, ESSEX

ISBN 1 872747 02 7

Design and Production: Colin Larkin
Editorial and production assistants:
Susan Pipe, Aileen Tyler, Pat Perry and Mustafa Sidki
This book has been produced on an Apple Macintosh IICX 8/80,
using Quark XPress 2.1 and Microsoft Word 4.
Image set in Monotype Classic Bembo by McNicol DataCom.
Cover printing by Technique
Printed and bound in England by Biddles Ltd

CONTENTS

ACKNOWLEDGEMENTS

The Leah Manning Trust gratefully acknowledges the work and time given by the Authors and the financial assistance from Harlow District Council, who made the publication of this book possible.

Special thanks to Barbara James for processing the words. George Taylor, A.R.P.S. for his photographic work. Leah's relatives for the loan of family photographs. The staffs of the following:

LIBRARIES
Bridgwater, Bristol, British Library, (Copyright, National Sound Archives and the Newspaper Libraries) Cambridge Collection, Droitwich, Greater London History, Guildhall (City of London), Hackney, Harlow, Islington, Labour Party, Marx Memorial, Salvation Army, Sunderland, Trades Union Congress, Westminster (Central Reference).

MUSEUMS
Bethnal Green Museum of Childhood, Harlow Museum, National Postal Museum, Victoria and Albert Museum.

RECORD OFFICES
Cambridge, Essex, Greater London, Hereford and Worcester, Somerset.Public Record Office, General Register Office (St. Catherines House).Hull University, (Dictionary of Labour Biography), London Borough of Richmond (Cemeteries Manager), Thanks to the National Union of Teachers and the Marx Memorial Library for use of archive material. To Victor Gollanz Ltd and Nockolds, Solicitors, for permission to use material and quotes from "A Life for Education" by Leah Manning 1970 (ISBN 0 575 00500 9). To the Christian Socialist Movement, Communist Party History Group, International Brigade Memorial Archive, the Harlow Gazette, Homerton College and Wansfell College.

PHOTOGRAPHIC PLATES:
Ron Bill: 2,4,5,8,9,10,11,12,14,16,17,18,19,22,34,41,47,48,55.
Cambridge Collection: 24,25. Victor Gollanz : 6,26,29,32,36,54. The Hulton Picture Company: 27,28,38,39,40,42. Marx Memorial Library: 30,33. National Union Of Teachers: 49. W.H. Palmer: 13. George Taylor A.R.P.S.: 51,52,53. Wansfell College: 31.

(We have been unable to trace the originators of some photographs used). The design of the birth, marriage and death certificates, Plates 1,20 and 50, are Crown Copyright and are reproduced with the permission of Her Majesty's Stationery Office.

FIGURES

A. The Song of the V.A.D.'s – by arrangement with the Cambridge Collection.

B,C,D,E, Newspaper extracts by arrangement with the British Library.

F, By arrangement with the Marx Memorial Library.

The authors would particularly like to thank Colin Larkin of Square One Books for professional and production advice during publication.

They also wish to thank the many individuals who assisted them including:

Don Anderson, Sonia Anderson, Tony Atienza, Joyce Bellamy, Barbara Castle, Kitty Clare, Peter Cope, Elvira Druce, John Druce, Dorothy Edwards, Major Jenty Fairbank, Doris G. Freeland, Ann Garner, Patt Gibberd, Beryl Gibbs, Livia Gollanz, John Gorman, Bob Guy, Pamela Heeks, Rev. D. Hodgson, Chris Morris, Rene Morris, Sandra Newens, Mr. C. W. Perrett, Sue Pipe, Mrs. J. Razey, Dr. O. Ross, Derek Score, Tom Skeffington-Lodge, Aileen Tyler, Betty Vernon, Irene Wagner, Kath White, Ron White, Joyce Woods.

All the documents and photographs collected during research for this book are to be deposited in the Essex Record Office.

PLATES

FOREWORD

When Leah's autobiography, "A Life For Education" was published in 1970, she was 84 years of age. At that time, she was still teaching and actively pursuing many of her lifelong interests. Her career in education and politics actually spanned 70 years of unparalleled economic, social, political and scientific change.

Her book describes her involvement in public work but skips over many aspects of her personal life. Research reveals, however, that the records do not entirely accord with Leah's recollections.

She says very little about her father and does not mention either his name or her own maiden name. According to her book, he was employed in her maternal grandfather's timber business and she recalls going out with him to estimate the value of standing timber.

In fact, her father, Charles William Perrett, throughout her life, down to his retirement, was a Captain in the Salvation Army, which he joined in his teens. His original trade was that of a baker and there is nothing to substantiate any active connection with the timber trade. Leah's parents did not emigrate to Canada in order to allow her father to exercise his expertise in timber, as she suggests ("A Life For Education" page 12), but to take up posts in the Salvation Army. Despite the fact that her marriage certificate [Plate 20] gives her father's occupation as that of a timber merchant, he was still an officer in the Salvation Army at the time of her wedding.

Leah refers to her "great grandmother," Susannah Tappin, who was apparently the subject of a short biography, "The King's Daughter," - not traced - which relates her work for the Primitive Methodist Chapel at Coopers Gardens in East London. She quotes her grandfather, George Tappin, as speaking of her as a wonderful mother, who was a member of a family of Huguenot immigrants.

Emma Susannah Rozee, to whom she refers, was in actuality not her great grandmother but her grandmother - the first wife of her grandfather, George Tappin. The latters mother, according to the record of his baptism on the 20th June 1826, was Mary Ann Tappin née Duff. His father, William Tappin, was, as Leah states, a silk weaver, but she confused his wife with his daughter-in-law.

As for her grandfather's re-marriage, which she says, occurred when she was four or five years old and caused a family crisis leading to several of her grandfather's children to emigrate, it appears that George Tappin and his second wife, Elizabeth, signed her parents' marriage certificate in 1884 – two years before she was born.

When Leah comes to her own marriage ("A Life For Education" Page 47) she says she became engaged early in 1914 and gives an account of how the growing crisis in Europe, of which she says she was only dimly aware, influenced this decision. Her husband-to-be told her they could not go to Germany for their honeymoon and they eventually settled for the Denver Regatta. The marriage certificate, [Plate 20], however, shows that the ceremony took place in July 1913 – not 1914. Her recollections of the Russian mobilisation and the assassination of Jaures must relate to her holiday a year later.

There are other discrepancies. John Underwood her great grandfather, whom she describes as a planter in Jamaica, with considerable business interests in Bristol, is given on his daughter's marriage certificate as a soldier and no evidence has come to light to substantiate the West Indian connection.

Again it has not proved possible to locate a birth or death certificate for the daughter she says she had and lost in infancy in 1918.

In Pamela Brookes' book, "Women at Westminster," it is stated that Leah "had been born in the United States" and this mistake appears elsewhere – even on her death certificate. [Plate 50]

Her birth certificate [Plate 1] makes it clear however that she first saw the light of day in Burrish Street, Droitwich, Worcestershire.[Plate 2]

In the face of such vagaries, it must be taken into account that on some matters of detail, her autobiography may not always be strictly accurate but of course other sources may also be flawed.

In the circumstances, it is unfortunate that she apparently destroyed her personal papers and records which might have shed light on the questions in doubt.

Nothing however, detracts from the basic achievements of Leah Manning. We have carefully researched all her public and personal activities and we believe that the work, which we have produced, rests on a firm foundation of fact and constitutes an accurate and a fitting tribute to a woman of quite outstanding quality.

During a long and industrious career, Leah Manning achieved distinction in many spheres but never attained the high public office for which she might have hoped. Even so, her contribution was remarkable in all the areas in which she was involved. Her life covered a period of dramatic change. Through two world wars, the General Strike, severe economic depression and post 1945 social revolution, she was in continuous activity.

Leah was a life-long campaigner for social and political causes from school milk in 1908 to anti-fascism in the 1930's and family planning in the 1960's. She had a considerable physical presence and a dominating personality, which she used to good effect in her political and wider public career.

She was one of a formidable generation of women who both individually and collectively made a major contribution to the political and social advances achieved during the first seventy years of this century. At this juncture, it is not easy fully to appreciate the obstacles faced by women as Britain emerged from the Victorian era. Leah and her feminist contemporaries – including women like Thelma Cazalet who stood as her Conservative opponent in the 1931 Islington East elections – had to fight for the right to vote, to enter Parliament to become J.P's and gain acceptance as equals. Once elected to Parliament, she battled on many issues raising the rights of women, including, equal pay for women teachers and civil servants, widows' pensions, Analgesia in childbirth, nurseries, woollen underwear, and the need for a Womens Rights Charter.

She was a determined, resolute and persistent advocate – always ready to help the humble and to do battle with the mighty. She was a doughty crusader in the cause of human advancement.

In 1980, Harlow District Council named a retired residents' day centre in her commemoration. [Plates 51-53]

The firm foundation, which has been established for basic social advance in our own day, which we must seek to defend and build upon, owes an immense amount to Leah and her contemporaries in the Labour movement. We should not forget such energy and endeavour but strive to emulate it in the times in which we live now.

RON BILL
STAN NEWENS

CHAPTER ONE
FAMILY AND CHILDHOOD

Elizabeth Leah Perrett, known in later life as Leah Manning, was born at Burrish Street, Droitwich, Worcestershire, on 14th April 1886. [Plate 2] (By a remarkable coincidence Manning Road adjoins Burrish Street). She was the first of twelve children, but only six survived to maturity, born to Charles William Perrett, a captain in the Salvation Army and his wife Harriet Margaret. [Plate 3] (See Family Tree pages 84 & 85).

Leah's father had been born in Bristol in 1862, the son of Thomas Laurence Perrett, a grocer and confectioner, trained originally as a baker. Thomas Laurence was the son of Samuel Perrett, a portrait painter and his wife Sarah Ann née Bennet. He became the husband of Thirza Bliss Underwood, the daugher of John Underwood, whose profession was given at the time as a soldier and at another as an accountant. According to Leah Manning, the latter became a Jamaican planter and died on a visit to Bristol accompanied by his two daughters, one of whom - at the tender age of 17 - promptly married Leah's grandfather - then aged 20.

Leah's aunt, her father's elder sister, Leah Selina Perrett, also became active in the Salvation Army and married a Salvation Army Adjutant, Thomas Martin. Another sister, Hettie Helena Perrett, married Walter Deacon. He was involved in business as a chemist and later became President of the Pharmaceutical Society of Great Britain. He was Mayor of Bridgwater in 1925, 1926 and 1927 and received the C.B.E. and the Freedom of Bridgwater. Another relative, Frank Perrett, lost his life in the First World War but left a son, Douglas Perrett, who was involved in business in Bridgwater down to the 1970's.

On her father's side, therefore, Leah Manning's family were well established in Bristol and Bridgwater. Perrett was in fact a familiar name in Somerset and surrounding areas and some of Leah's relatives claimed descent from a Norman baron, Henry Perret, who was said to have settled there. They also asserted that the River Parret, on which Bridgwater stands, derived its name from the same origin.

Unlike any of these, Leah Manning's mother came from East London. Born in 1863 in Castle Street, Bethnal Green, Harriet Margaret Tappin was a teacher before her marriage, the daughter of George Tappin, a timber merchant, who later moved out to Pownall Road, Hackney, and finally to a pleasant spacious house known as "Hillside", 4, Osbaldeston Road, Stoke Newington. [Plates 4 & 5].

George Tappin was one of the sons of William Tappin, a silk weaver, who had married Mary Ann Duff at St. Dunstan's Church, Stepney in 1822. He was baptised at St. Leonard's Church, Shoreditch in 1826.

George married Emma Susannah Rozee, the daughter of George Rozee, a silk weaver, whose forebears were Huguenots. According to Leah Manning, she was a descendant of silk merchants in Lyons who fled to England to escape religious persecution, after Louis XIV revoked the Edict of Nantes which had guaranteed freedom of worship to French Protestants. (Tappin may also be a Huguenot name as the records mention an earlier Pierre Tappin). Emma Susannah Rozee already had a daughter – also Emma Susannah Rozee – when she married in 1846. She went on to have two sons and several additional daughters, of whom Harriet Margaret was one.

Susan Tappin, [Plate 6] as she was known, became an active member of the Primitive Methodists at their first London Chapel which stood just to the north of St. Leonard's Church, Shoreditch, in an alley called Coopers Gardens. The original building was no more than 20 feet square but contained three galleries. It was rebuilt three times and served for many years as the centre of their work in the metropolis. The story of Susan Tappin was told, according to Leah Manning, in a brief biography, "The King's Daughter," a copy of which she treasured throughout her life.

The area to the south of Coopers Gardens was the site of one of the most notorious slums in London – the Old Nicholl, which featured in the writings of a succession of commentators, most notably a few years later, in Arthur Morrison's well known novel: "A Child of the Jago." Amidst poverty, filth, overcrowding, crime and immorality, Susan Tappin handed out religious tracts, relieved those in need, delivered the children of the poor and practised her faith. In defiance of public smears, threats of violence and killer diseases, she remained true to her beliefs in her day-to-day conduct as well as her worship as long as she lived. She was called "The King's Daughter," after standing up to someone who insulted her when she attempted to give him a tract. Her example was an important influence on her family – not least on

Leah Manning - despite the fact that the latter did not see the light of day until her grandmother, who died at the early age of 46 in 1871, had been dead some fifteen years.

A common religious faith was apparently responsible for bringing Leah Manning's parents together. Her father joined the Bristol III Corps of the Salvation Army and, in 1882, at 19 years of age, left his native city to go to the Salvation Army Training House. From there he was appointed to the Poplar Corps and he was subsequently sent to open a Corps at South Hornsey. Harriet Margaret Tappin became a member of the South Hornsey Corps. She left it to go to the Training Home in January 1884 and was subsequently appointed to Widnes. The couple must, however, have remained in touch for in December 1884, they were married in Peterborough.

In her early childhood, Leah Manning may have returned with her parents to Bridgwater and attended St.John's School, Bridgwater. However, in the early 1890's Charles and Harriet Perrett agreed to go to Canada to carry on their work for the Salvation Army and Leah went to live with her maternal grandfather, George Tappin and his second wife at Osbaldeston Road, Stoke Newington.

Leah says that her parents emigrated to America when she was in her teens. but it appears however that they went first to Canada where her father took up a Salvation Army post. They probably moved on to America around 1910. Some of her brothers and sisters accompanied their parents but two sons, Charles and Lawrence, stayed behind, although the latter rejoined them in 1914 or thereabouts. Leah's father's final assignment as a Salvation Army Officer was in Rochford, Illinois, where he died. Here his wife finally retired.

George Tappin and his wife, with whom Leah went to live after her parents left Britain, had several sons and daughters but two of the latter, Elizabeth and Susan had apparently emigrated with their husbands and children to Australia and New Zealand, before Harriet Margaret went to Canada. Though his sons George and Joseph remained with him until they were married and then carried on in the timber trade in East London, Leah Manning's grandfather must have felt a deep sense of loss. She was left with the impression that her aunts left because they resented their stepmother. Perhaps the loss of his daughters overseas explains the deep love and care which he lavished on his granddaughter to whom he undoubtedly transmitted many of the beliefs that he had shared with his first wife, Emma Susannah.

Though George Tappin was a staunch and unwavering Methodist with a puritanical faith, he was also a Liberal and a radical; for him the politics of Gladstone and his successors in the Liberal party followed automatically from the teachings of his church. Inevitably, Leah, who adored him, was deeply influenced. She was in addition affected by the books provided for her by her step grandmother, which emphasised faith, temperance and morality but also compassion for the victims of poverty and misfortune. Stories like the Basket of Flowers, Jessica's First Prayers, and Christie's Old Organ gripped her imagination even though they came in for criticism from David, her step-mother's son, who was only a few years older than she. His attitude to some extent counter balanced the strict religious atmosphere which otherwise tended to surround her at this formative period of her life and, at his suggestion, she read Sir Walter Scott and Charles Dickens. Some of the embarrassing questions she asked at times were probably stimulated by this connection.

Life was, however, sheltered and comfortable by and large. On summer days, the family would enjoy outings in the brake to Theydon Bois, where 40 years on,Leah would be establishing a temporary home for some of the refugee children she brought to England to escape the Spanish Civil War.

David's decision, which she did not fully understand at the time, to join the army and fight for South Africa, despite her grandfather's sympathy for the Boers, who were fighting for their independence, therefore came as a great shock. His subsequent death at the siege of Mafeking caused her endless grief and pushed her decisively in the direction of pacifism which influenced her throughout her life.

When Leah went to live with her grandfather, she was, after a period, sent to the Misses Thorns Select Academy for Young Ladies. She did not, however, take to this and transferred to a different school. By chance, this brought her into contact with the Reverend Stewart Headlam [Plate 7] when he was visiting as a member of the London School Board.He was a controversial priest who opposed church schools, campaigned for the repeal of the Blasphemy Act and urged the nationalisation of land. He supported the theatre, the music hall, the ballet and the pub. It was his support for these activities that in 1878 led to his removal from the curacy of St. Matthews, Bethnal Green. [Plate 8] He was one of the founders - and the driving force, of the Guild of St. Matthew, founded the previous year and the most influential Christian Socialist organisation of the time. It had been formed by a group of young parishioners entirely concerned with what they regarded as the all important rite of the church - holy communion. However, it also included the objective of "promoting the study of social and political questions in the light of the Incarnation. " Stewart Headlam said the last six words were the "raison d'etre" of Christian Socialism and all the efforts towards social and political reform. Although its maximum membership was only 333 in 1894 it was a very influential organisation. However the Guild declined around the turn of the century and it was gradually succeeded by the Christian Social Union. The Guild was finally dissolved in 1909. Stewart Headlam died on 18th November 1924 aged 77. His gravestone [Plate 9] in East Sheen Cemetery, Richmond, Surrey, is inscribed: "He devoted his life and dauntless ability to the welfare of the children, students and teachers in our London schools by whom he was affectionately revered as was none other."

A memorial service was held in St. Martins-in-the-Fields. The London County Council commemorated him in Bethnal Green by Stewart Headlam School and Headlam Street. [Plate 10] A memorial plaque was placed on his former residence in Wilmot Street. Stewart Headlam not only encouraged Leah in her studies but, to the horror of her strictly puritanical grandparents, introduced her to the theatre. Leah was captivated. When she matriculated, he helped to find her a post as a pupil teacher at Oldfield Road School [Plate 11] and gave her two books to read: The Socialist Church and The Meaning of Mass. Though his high-church leanings were strongly at variance with the outlook of her grandfather, they, perhaps unknowingly, held similar views on Oscar Wilde. Stewart Headlam stood bail for him whilst Leah recalls the family discussing the vicious sentence he received. Leah began to attend services at St. Margaret's Church, Westminster, [Plate 12] the Church of Parliament, where Stewart Headlam preached. Some forty years later, as an M.P., she would be a member of its Parliamentary Church Council. Her Christian Socialist principles and commitment- derived from this formative period - were strongly held and observed, throughout her life.

She now hoped to enter a university, but before she could obtain a place, her grandfather died. As his sons had all married and moved away, her step-grandmother decided that the house was too big for Leah and herself and an elderly relative who lived with them. She therefore made arrangements to move to Hampshire. On Stewart Headlam's advice, Leah applied to attend Homerton Teacher Training College, Cambridge [Plate ...] and was given a place after passing the entrance examination.

CHAPTER TWO
CAMBRIDGE DAYS AND THE N.U.T.

In her book, Leah says "Cambridge enchanted me." Indeed her description of the joy and emotion she felt is the most lyrical passage of "A Life For Education."

"Love affairs are ephemeral things. They come and they go... But a love affair with a place is forever; it is love at first sight: it can span half a century, the image growing ever deeper and always more fair than on that first day. It was my startled glance out of the staircase window, on my way down to Hall the next morning, (after the entrance examination interview) that began my love affair with Cambridge. Anyone who has seen a fen sunrise or sunset can never forget it... I had always thought that Turner's vivid landscapes had lived only in his imagination, or must have been an exaggeration. But here was exaggeration of an exaggeration – the whole sky was on fire– no sky, no blue, no clouds, just a sweep of crimson, gold and flame, dying away as I stood there, to a faint daffodil yellow."

After the exam she walked around the city "till I came at last to rest in Kings Chapel. Awed by its beauty, I knelt and prayed that I might come to this perfect place to live for three years. I did not guess, then, that I would live there for half a century and do my best work there."

In those next three years of her life, 1906-1908, Leah studied, swam, played tennis and hockey, made friends and enjoyed college life: She became chairman of a debating society and a drama club, secretary of the Student Christian Union and took the initiative in forming the Socialist League which Stewart Headlam came to address. She also met Hugh Dalton, the future Labour Cabinet Minister, who became a lifelong friend. After being introduced by Hugh Dalton, she joined the University Fabian Society and in due course the Cambridge Independent Labour Party.

In the third volume of his biography "High Tide and After" he recounts that after his resignation as Chancellor in 1947, he made an assignation with Leah to sit beside her on the third bench below the gangway. We were both rabble rousers at Cambridge he wrote.

After satisfactorily completing her final examinations, she was miserable at the thought of leaving Cambridge. She recounts "wandering round all my favourite haunts and for the last time having tea at Buols with a few of my boyfriends." Buols at 17, Kings Parade [Plate 14] faced her favourite building, Kings Chapel, which she always visited when in the city. [Plate 15].

However, to her surprise, she was offered – and dubiously accepted, a post at the College practice school at New Street, in an impoverished and unfashionable area of the city. Her stay in Cambridge eventually lasted another twenty five years. At the appointment interviews she met Dora Burman and afterwards they had tea at The Dorothy in Hobson Street. [Plate 16]. On a joint income of £117 per annum they found a four roomed flat in Granchester Street for £1 per week rent. [Plate 17]

From there Leah had a "pleasant early morning bicycle ride in the softly-rising morning mists, across Coe Fen and down Silver Street." [Plate 18].

At New Street School, she was in charge of a class of 70/80 mostly ragged, poor, cold and hungry working class children, who lived within a stone's throw of world famous seats of learning. The school had been founded in 1846 to provide undenominational education to the children of Barnwell. Its location in a very poor and neglected part of the town led to it being called the "Ragged School." It was supervised by an uncertificated mistress until 1885 when Mr. W.T. Haynes became the first Headmaster. The school continued to expand and additional infant accommodation was added in 1885 and 1893, by 1901 187 children were on the role.

In 1898 the Managers prepared a further development scheme to provide accommodation for older boys and girls. However, they were unable to raise sufficient funds and, after protracted negotiations, a scheme of co-operation was agreed with Homerton College. This provided that the Trustees and Managers provided the site, the scholars and the teaching staff, whilst the College would meet the cost of the buildings and have the right to use the whole school for the practice of their students. The extension, accommodating 294 pupils, was opened by the Mayor, Alderman H.M. Taylor, on 7th February 1901. The commemorative plaque [Plate 19] records the event – but curiously gives no date.

She was soon campaigning for school meals and school milk and came into the public eye for her bitter denunciation of the death of an underfed child, for which she was summoned to appear before the Education Committee. After a visit to the United States to see her parents, she secured the support of several teaching colleagues and Mrs. Keynes of the National Council of Women to launch an "After School Play Centre" at New Street

School. This won her support from a wide spectrum of the community .

In July 1913, Leah married [Plate 20] William Henry Manning, [Plate 21] an assistant at the University Solar Physics Observatory, the son of a Fenland market gardener, Joseph Manning, and a Liberal in politics. Initially they lived in Bridge Street but later moved to a house at the Solar Physics Laboratory [Plate 22] in Madingley Road. Will stayed there until at least 1949 –Leah is not listed after 1934, but certainly spent many weekends in Cambridge.

Leah had expected to resign her teaching post as was customary upon marriage but the outbreak of the First World War gave her the opportunity to carry on. Though opposed to the war, (as were her fellow members of the I.L.P.), she volunteered as a Voluntary Aid Detachment (V.A.D.) [Plate 23] at the The First Eastern General Hospital. The hospital, between Burrells Walk and West Road, had been mobilised on the fifth of August 1914 and received its first patients less than three weeks later on sixteenth August. Over the next four years it dealt with many thousands of injured servicemen.

The V.A.D.s had their own song:-

The Song of the V.A.D.'s
Tune, "Tipperary". Time, 7.30 a.m.
It's a big, big rush to the cloakroom,
It's a big, big rush to go;
It's a big, big crush in the cloakroom,
It's the biggest crush I know.
Good–bye to all neatness,
Farewell, tidy hair;
It's a big, big rush to the cloakroom,
But we all get there.
    ONE OF THEM
(reprinted from FIRST EASTERN GENERAL HOSPITAL [CAMBRIDGE] GAZETTE 7/12/1915).

She became a member of the Insurance Committee at Cambridge and later Secretary of the Borough Food Control Committee. Her husband was away for much of the time on war work and between times Leah continued to organise and attend political meetings in the Cambridge area. In 1915 she mourned the death of Rupert Brooke – a friend from college days. She probably overworked and lost her first and only child who, born in the summer of 1918, died three weeks afterwards. Thereafter she threw herself anew into political work.

Leah remained at New Street School although the war had caused the ending of the After School scheme due to blackout problems. Near to the end of the war she became acting Head of a large girls' school whilst the headmistress was on sick leave. When that appointment concluded she took charge of Vinery Road Open Air School. This had been established in 1916 with 30 children, in a cottage and garden in Vinery Road. Leah had studied Open Air Schools in Germany and America and was well qualified for this new post. In 1920 the school was enlarged by two huts purchased from the army. However the Borough wanted a new purpose built school and purchased four acres of land in Ascham Road for this purpose. The scheme was delayed by economy measures and the foundation stone was not laid until 12th May 1927. The school opened as Milton Road Open Air School the following year – with the official ceremony performed by Sir Humphry Rolleston on 7th July. Leah was the first headmistress, [Plate 24] a post she held until her entry to Parliament in 1931. These posts provided a base for her continuing activities in education and politics.

In February 1917 a Revolution took place in Russia, followed in October by the triumph of the Bolsheviks under Lenin. Leah welcomed the end of the Czarist autocracy. In November 1918 the German authorities accepted an armistice and she rejoiced at the return of peace. She was then Chairman of the Cambridge Trades Council and the Labour Party. She attended the Labour Party Conference in November and returned to Cambridge full of enthusiasm for the forthcoming General Election. She was determined that both Cambridge seats should be contested by a Labour candidate for the first time and rushed around to help bring this about.

In the event, the Party put forward the Reverend Rhonnda Williams, a Non-Conformist Minister, for the City, and Albert Stubbs, a printing worker and longstanding member locally, for Cambridgeshire County. The committee rooms were in Regent Street. Speakers at meetings included Sidney Webb, Professor Hobson and Margaret Macmillan. The public were, however, in an unsympathetic jingoistic mood and all the self-sacrifice of the Cambridge Party was to no avail.

The results were deeply disappointing:

CITY

Rt. Hon. Sir Eric Geddes (Con.)	11553
Rev. T. Rhonnda Williams (Lab.)	3789

COUNTY

Rt. Hon. E.S. Montague (Lib.)	12497
A.E. Stubbs (Lab.)	6686

Leah's personal problems were compounded by the fact that her husband was a staunch Liberal and worked for the Rt.Hon. E.S. Montague. They had to avoid the chance of a personal confrontation during the course of the campaign.

Nothing daunted, she carried on. Shortly after the armistice, she accepted an invitation from Wilfred Wellock, Secretary of the Fellowship of Reconciliation, to visit Germany where the Quakers had established a camp at Wansee, near Berlin. There she met German socialists including one of the truly outstanding figures of the Left and a consistent opponent of the war, Rosa Luxemburg. Sadly Rosa Luxemburg was murdered within months in January 1919. Leah, however,kept up her connections and returned to Germany nearly every year until the advent of Hitler to power in 1933.

She also went to America to see her family during this period of her life. This gave her a profound interest in international affairs and broadened the dimensions of her Socialist convictions.

In no way, however, did it diminish her activity on the home front. She was a member of the Labour Party Advisory Committee on Education. In 1917 H.A.L. Fisher, President of the Board of Education said that;- "An anxious and depressed teacher is a bad teacher, an embittered teacher is a social danger . . . the first condition of educational advance is that we should learn to pay our teachers better." Leah supported the Fisher Act of 1918 and spoke at many public meetings supporting its objectives. In Cambridge, she helped Hugh Dalton to become the prospective Labour Party Parliamentary Candidate and worked hard for him in the Cambridge 1922 by-Election. The result was :-

Sir Douglas Newton (Con)	10867
Hugh Dalton (Lab)	6954

On this occasion Will was persuaded to vote for Hugh. However, Labour not unexpectedly failed to win the seat.

In 1920 Leah together with Mrs. Bethune Baker and Miss J.Harrison were appointed as J.P.'s for the City in the first list of women justices in the country. At the swearing-in, on 23rd August 1920, [Plate 25], the Mayor said they were making history and it would be interesting to see if they would be less severe on sentencing offenders. She refused however to let this public office inhibit her other activities, even during the General Strike from 3rd to

12th May 1926 when she played a leading part in the Cambridge Council of Action. She helped to organise domestic workers – 'The Bedders', [Plate 26] laundry workers and other women employees, in trade unions. She took part in an unsuccessful campaign to unionise the Chivers Jam Factory at Histon, after the management locked in their workers – mainly women – during the mid-day break. She also fought several unsuccessful battles to win a seat on Cambridgeshire County Council.

Leah had for some years been a staunch member of the National Union of Teachers. This led to her election as Secretary of the Cambridge Borough Teachers Association and Secretary to the Joint Advisory Committee to the Local Education Authority. Later she became a Member of the Joint Employment Committee and the Cambridgeshire Joint Scholarship Board.

Her education travels at this time took her to Amsterdam, Budapest and Geneva. In 1924 she was elected to the N.U.T. Executive and became Chairman of the N.U.T. Law Committee and a Member of the Burnham Committee (the latter after many threats over the years, was abolished by the Education Act of 1987). In 1926 she was awarded a scholarship for a lecture tour of the United States from the Womens' Club of America, given through the English Speaking Union – of which Leah had been a founder member.

She wrote a regular column in the School Mistress for a number of years. She also associated with the "forward" movement in the Union which was left-wing or liberal in politics and she worked closely with figures like W.G. Cove (President of the N.U.T. in 1922 and later a Labour M.P.), W.W. Hill (President in 1928) and Frederick Mander (later General Secretary). In April 1930 she was elected President at the N.U.T. Diamond Jubilee Conference at Bournemouth – the fourth woman to have achieved this distinction and a well-deserved recognition of her contribution to education.

Leah was reported as controlling the Conference with "efficiency, charm and dignity." Her Presidential Address concentrated on the raising of the school leaving age, to 15, and the provision of new secondary schools. She argued for an end of surging materialism and pleaded for:-
"a great 20th Century renaissance which will give education an absolute value, because education is life. A recovery of faith in the value of life, of the potential, perchance unique, value of each individual life."

At the Conference dinner, Leah records that she listened enthralled to Sir Meredith Whittaker (born 1840) proposing the toast of "Education" with Gladstonian gesture, diction, wit and wisdom. She remarked afterwards that:-
"whilst violently disagreeing with most of what he said, nothing I have

ever heard has taught me more thoroughly what 1870 meant to those who took part in the struggle."

During the Conference Leah had agreed to speak to the Co-operative Congress at York and, because of Bank Holiday traffic, only managed the return trip by chartering an aeroplane. After the address at 11.30, Leah got back to Scarborough for lunch. She was very impressed and suggested that perhaps the union should provide the President with an aeroplane! Over the years Leah flew many thousands of miles. She once said that she spent her time looking at the tiny windows and wondering how she would squeeze through in an emergency.

As N.U.T. President, Leah visited the House of Commons in June 1930 to listen to the debate on the Second Reading of the Education Bill. She described how the men in the group were accommodated in the Distinguished Strangers' Gallery in the coveted seats "Under the Gallery" whilst she and her colleague Miss Conway were relegated to the Members' Gallery. Leah protested vigorously about the legend that no woman could be a Distinguished Stranger because apparently they could not be trusted not to speak! She said afterwards" It is time these futile restrictions were ended."

As President of the Union she travelled incessantly and spent enormous amounts of time negotiating with civil servants and officials about salaries, religious instruction in schools and other issues. Her period of office coincided with the second Labour Government, in which Sir Charles Trevelyan, as President of the Board of Education, tried to introduce a Bill to raise the school-leaving age to 15. This was defeated in the Lords eventually and the Minister resigned. Leah Manning was deeply involved in discussions about the bill before this occurred and Sir Charles Trevelyan also appointed her to a Departmental Committee which was considering private schools. Together with chairing Executive meetings and the Unions' National Conference, she found her hands full during the Presidential Year.

At this stage in her career she finally decided she would seek to enter the House of Commons. Previously she had declined requests to allow her name to go forward. When, however, she was approved by the Union of Post Office Workers to seek the nomination at Bristol East, where their sponsored M.P. Walter Baker, was seriously ill and not expected to live, she accepted the offer. She had already been nominated for the N.U.T. Parliamentary List – the first woman ever – and the sponsorship carried with it some financial backing for any campaign which she fought. Her entry, on to the Parliamentary stage as the Member of Parliament for Bristol East appeared to be only a matter of time.

CHAPTER THREE
ISLINGTON EAST ELECTIONS 1931

Walter Baker, Labour M.P. for Bristol East, had died at the end of 1930, just after Sir James Melville the Labour Solicitor General had resigned owing to ill-health, and a promising young lawyer, Stafford Cripps, had been appointed in his place. Unfortunately he was not a Member of Parliament. Arthur Henderson M.P. who was Secretary and Treasurer to the Labour Party, decided that the Bristol by-election would be the ideal opportunity for Sir Stafford (newly knighted) to enter the House of Commons.

Leah Manning was furious and at first refused to give way. Eventually however, pressurised by the Labour Party Establishment through her old friend Hugh Dalton M.P. - then Under Secretary-of-State at the Foreign Office - Leah withdrew with bad grace. The second Labour Government was facing very serious problems and she did not wish to seem more concerned about herself than the Party. However, she never forgave Cripps and was still prepared to denigrate him forty years later when she wrote her autobiography.

Early in 1931 however, Dr. Ethel Bentham, Labour M.P. for Islington East died. She had shared Leah's interests in under-nourished children in Cambridge and both had been appointed J.P's for the Borough in 1920. Dr. Bentham had been Labour M.P. for Islington East since 1918. Her sudden death after a short illness in January 1931 saddened her friend and caused the by-election which gave Leah her first Parliamentary term. In return for Leah's loyalty over Bristol, Arthur Henderson had promised her the next by-election. On 19th January 1931, Leah was in Wellingborough for the first Annual Dinner of the local N.U.T. She received an urgent message to return to London. Henderson brow beat the Islington East Constituency Labour Party - who initially did not want a "school-marm" - with the same insensitivity that he had employed against Bristol East C.L.P. - who had not wanted a rich man, i.e. Sir Stafford Cripps. Again Arthur Henderson got his way and on the following Wednesday, 28th January, Leah was selected as Labour candidate - the first woman Parliamentary candidate to be sponsored by the N.U.T. She spent the first few days contacting people in social, political and religious life – including Donald Soper. Islington was, she said, not a typical London Borough but "had a soul and personality of its own."

She wrote afterwards that "the weather was bitingly cold," but on the day following the election the Guardian was still able to report that: –"She emerged from the battle looking as fresh as paint."

It was a hard fought contest that Labour hardly expected to win, but Leah was victorious – largely owing to the intervention of an Empire Crusade candidate, backed by Lord Beaverbrook, which split the Conservative vote.

Indeed, it was Lord Beaverbrook himself who opened the campaign at Islington Town Hall on Friday, 30th January 1931 with a speech supporting the prospective Empire Crusade candidate Mr. P. E. Springham. He later withdrew from the campaign, however, after pledging his support for Miss Cazalet. However, the susbsequent adoption of Brigadier General A.C. Critchley, Managing Director of The Greyhound Racing Association and a Director of British Portland Cement, as the Empire Crusade candidate ensured that the Conservative vote would still be split. Major H.E. Crawfurd, AFC, who had been M.P. for Walthamstow from 1924–1929, was the Liberal standard bearer.

The official Conservative candidate was Miss Thelma Cazalet, a London County Councillor. Her brother, Victor Cazalet, was Tory M.P. for Chippenham.

Thelma Cazalet and Leah were both descendants of Huguenot refugee families who left France after the revocation of the Edict of Nantes. Both were members of the Womens Freedom League. The League wanted women "to use the power of the Parliamentary vote" (women over 21 were only enfranchised in 1928) "to elect women to Parliament and other public bodies, to establish equality of rights and opportunities between the sexes and to promote the social and industrial well being of the community." Sixty years later many of its aims remain unfulfilled. Despite their political differences, Leah and Thelma had many similar interests.

Miss Cazalet's mother had been involved with the Pankhursts and the Webbs and Thelma had attended Fabian lectures by Shaw and Webb. Although losing to Leah in the by-election, she reversed the result in the October General Election and remained M.P. for Islington East until defeated in 1945 –when Leah returned to the Commons as M.P. for Epping.

Like Leah, Thelma was a frequent parliamentary speaker on education matters and an early advocate of comprehensive schools. In 1937 she was the first woman to be appointed as a Parliamentary Private Secretary - to the Parliamentary Secretary to the Board of Education, becoming Secretary herself in the 1945 Caretaker Government.

She was an ardent feminist and a lifelong campaigner for womens' rights. In 1944 she played a significant part in Winston Churchill's decision to establish a Royal Commission on Equal Pay. In 1947 she was Chairman of the Equal Pay Campaign. After a long public career she died at the age of 89 on 13th January 1989.

On Nomination day, Tuesday 10th February 1931, the four candidates were duly registered for the Election on Thursday 19th. The second week of the campaign saw over 120 indoor and a large number of outdoor meetings held throughout the constituency. The liveliest and rowdiest of these were reported to be those at which Lord Beaverbrook spoke. At a Conservative rally, Lord Hailsham enraged at Beaverbrook's intervention, said: "Lord Beaverbrook comes to East Islington and is compared to an elephant trumpeting in the jungle or a man-eating tiger. I am inclined to compare him with a mad dog running along the streets and yapping and barking. I would remind his Lordship that the best way to treat a mad dog if you cannot muzzle him is to shoot him."

Leah, meanwhile, concentrated on the issues of unemployment, food, education, peace, prices, housing, Trade Union rights and shorter working hours and improving the quality of life for the working class. The Labour Government had, she declared;- "increased unemployment benefit, increased the numbers entitled to benefit, removed the 'not genuinely seeking work' clause. Its 1930 Housing Act provides the chance for a vigorous attack on the slums of our Country, I range myself with the Government and the Trade Union movement in demanding the restoration of full Trade Union rights."

Leah became a favourite in the constituency during the campaign and became known as "dearie" or "gal". Her only real dislike during the campaign was the photographers; they followed her canvassing rounds and she hated them. "I'm the world's worst subject for photographs", she declared, Speakers supporting her during the campaign included Philip Snowden, A.V. Alexander, George Lansbury, Susan Lawrence, Reg Sorensen, Ernest Bevin and Philip Noel-Baker. The short frenetic campaign came to a climax on polling day Thursday, 19th February 1931. It was the usual strenuous day of visiting Committee Rooms and encouraging party workers.

Leah was the first candidate to arrive at the count, the first to be held in the new Town Hall. She wrote afterwards of it being "one long agony." Outside a huge crowd of over 5,000 people had gathered with Labour supporters repeatedly singing "The Red Flag." After the announcement of the result in the Hall and the usual thanks and formalities the Mayor proceeded to the Town Hall steps to give the result to the waiting crowds. Leah said later, "I don't remember being more truly frightened in the whole of my life." She appeared with a bouquet of red and yellow tulips and with a triumphant smile addressed the crowd;- "My friends, I desire to thank you for the magnificent victory you have accorded the Government tonight - a victory in favour of keeping the standard of life of the working class as high as ever. I hope to represent all classes of Islington East with impartiality and to be a friend of this Constituency as Dr. Ethel Bentham was." Women dashed from the crowd to kiss her and the mounted police had to clear a way for her car through the mass of supporters.Leah commented;- "I have emerged happy, victorious and unscathed, yet in spite of all my hard work not one ounce less". Despite a hectic, noisy, vigorous and well publicised by-election only 50.1% of the electorate voted, compared to 66% in 1929. The respective results were:-

1929

Dr. Ethel Bentham	(Lab)	15199
Major R. Tasker	(Con)	13641
Mr. E. Middleton	(Lib)	11136
Majority:		1558

1931 (19th February 1931).

Mrs. L. Manning	(Lab)	10591
Brig.Gen. A.C. Critchley	(Empire Crusade)	8314
Miss T. Cazalet	(Con)	7182
Major Crawfurd	(Lib)	4450
Majority:		2277

As the result was declared at Islington her father-in-law was dying in Cambridge - but he died "proud of her - knew she would do it."

An interesting social statistic records that the electoral register for that election contained 33,443 women and 27,083 men. She wrote in the March issue of Labour Magazine that the main issues had been the wages threat and the restoration of trade union rights.

During the campaign, Leah wrote that she was impressed by the intelligent nature of the questions put by women and encouraged by the fact that women who had initially shown little interest were becoming keen on political matters. Leah was described as the first "working class mother" to sit in the House. This contrasts with Stewart Headlam's note to Hugh Dalton suggesting he should contact her when she became a student at Homerton

College. It said she was "from a rather stuffy middle-class family." This of course referred to her grandfather's house at Stoke Newington where the area – and domestic staff – certainly suggested a middle-class environment.

Leah was proud to take her place with other women colleagues in the House, including Dr. Marion Phillips, Susan Lawrence, Mary MacArthur, Margaret Bondfield, Ellen Wilkinson, Lucy Noel-Buxton, Cynthia Mosley and Jennie Lee.

Her Maiden speech on 9th March 1931, was in a debate on International Arbitration, and the proposed Accession to chapters 1-4 of the League of Nations' proposals for the settlement of disputes. Leah said:– "I feel that it is not inappropriate for a newly elected woman Member of this House, in addressing the House of Commons for the first time, to speak upon a subject of such vital importance to the women of the world as that which is laid before the House tonight . . . my voice is enlarged and enhanced by the feeling and aspiration of thousands of women outside this House. Women, especially, have a passionate anxiety that the Foreign Secretary should succeed in that path which he has carved out for the nation, the path which will lead to a day when the world shall know war no more."

At a public meeting supporting Arthur Henderson's proposals for a World Disarmament Conference, she expressed the hope that Britain might undertake disarmament by example instead of waiting for disarmament by agreement.

She naturally took a particular interest in education and kept in close touch with the N.U.T. Headquarters. According to an interview with Bernard Donoughue and C.W.Jones, biographers of Herbert Morrison, Leah was approached by J.H.Thomas to take a Junior post at the Board of Education, but did not accept. She campaigned for Family Allowances and was appointed to a Select Committee considering the hours of work and conditions of shop assistants. She was however quite hurt by the unfriendly disposition of Jimmy Maxton and other former I.L.P. colleagues. On free Saturday afternoons she would have a guest seat in the Directors Box at Highbury to watch Arsenal play.

In 1931, she also spoke in a debate on the Cathedral Measures – Church of England Assembly Powers:– "I would have thought that the right hon. Gentleman (Lord H. Cecil, Oxford University) would have inserted in that Clause some facilities for the appointment of women as bishops. It is a matter of deep disappointment to me that, when this matter comes before the House, we should find the Noble Lord recalcitrant in regard to the question of women in the Church and their preferment to positions to which they have a perfect right, and where I am sure they could perform their duties to the glory of God just as well as the bishops. It is a matter of deep disappointment to me to find that women are not included."

However, the Labour Government was in deep crisis over the economic situation and, within months, a majority of the cabinet refused to support the drastic cuts in public expenditure recommended by the May Committee, leaving the Prime Minister in a minority. Ramsay MacDonald forced his opponents to resign and formed a National Government with Liberal and Conservative co-operation. On 7th November when the Labour Party Annual Conference was in session at Scarborough, the news came through that Parliament had been dissolved.

In a little over seven months, fortunes were reversed. The General Election on 27th October 1931 ended Leah's short sojourn as an M.P. and Thelma Cazalet was elected National Conservative M.P. for Islington East.

On nomination day, 16th October, it emerged that the election would be a straight fight between the two ladies. [Plate 27]. In her endorsement speech Leah said:- "We shall make this a fight for wages and food. Labour is out to protect the worker and his wife."

It was another short campaign. [Plate 28]. The candidates became the centre of attraction to awaiting newsmen and both were filmed and interviewed on the steps of the Town Hall. Labour set up their Committee Rooms in St. Paul's Road and displayed an illuminated board outside with the legend:- "Mrs. Manning's record will bear the light."

On Tuesday 20th October the candidates spoke to the Chamber of Commerce at Beale's Restaurant in Holloway Road. Leah spoke at over 50 indoor meetings during the campaign including at Salters Hall, at the Mildmay Radical Club and at Johnson Hall, Ronalds Road. She again concentrated on the family and social issues. She deplored the cuts in education spending and the salary reductions for teachers, civil servants and other public employees and the reduction in unemployment benefit. She quoted the hardship that local people were representing to her - and gave the example of a man, wife and two children receiving 27/9d a week with £1 to pay for rent. She continued:- "I say with no uncertain voice that you cannot vote for anybody who does not understand and realise the conditions of life of the poorest in the community. I say to you that as you are your brother's keeper you dare not vote for such a policy."

The electorate did not share this view and after a campaign in which it was glibly assailed, by its former leaders -James Ramsay MacDonald, Philip Snowdon and J.H. Thomas - the Labour Party was devastated by the loss of

243 of its 289 seats - including Islington East.

The result was:-

Miss T. Cazalet	(Con.)	27,221
Mrs. L. Manning	(Lab.)	13,111

Leah, who had automatically supported the Party found herself out of office and out of work. What made the defeat even more galling, at the personal level, was the news that Bristol East, the constituency which she had given up for Sir Stafford Cripps, had stayed Labour.

Fortunately the N.U.T. was looking for a new Assistant Education Officer and she secured the post. Although re-adopted as "prospective" Labour candidate for the seat, she found that her financial commitment to the Islington East party was taking much of her N.U.T. salary and eventually in 1933 she resigned.

A year before this at the Leicester Labour Party Conference in 1932 Leah had lost the seat she won on the National Executive Committee in 1931. She attributed this to her membership of a sub-committee on banking, chaired by Hugh Dalton, which failed to recommend nationalisation of the joint-stock banks. Sir Frederick Mander, General Secretary of the NUT, now opposed her standing for Parliament again on the grounds that the responsibilities would clash with her duties as Assistant Education Officer. She declined possible nomination at Darlington -to face Harold MacMillan - on the grounds that it was too far from London. She consulted the National Agent at Transport House who came up with the suggestion of sharing the two member constituency of Sunderland. The other Labour candidate was D.N. Pritt. Surprisingly, so soon after her resignation at Islington East, she decided to accept.

In the event it proved to be a trying experience for her.

CHAPTER FOUR
THE 1935 GENERAL ELECTION

After her selection as a prospective candidate for Sunderland Leah spent many weeks motoring to and from London, attending both party and public meetings and standing on the terraces at Roker Park to support Sunderland Football Club. She recalled that both she and Johnny Pritt were confident of victory right up to the announcement of the election, and the emergence of a revised opposition team.

Labour and the Liberals had a "local understanding" in Sunderland which enabled them to sustain an anti Tory majority on the local Council. Labour thought that this understanding (on tactical candituring!) would extend to the General Election in order to maximise the opposition to the National Tory combination. However the Conservative Central Office persuaded one of the Tory candidates to stand down and be substituted by Mr. S.N. Furness, a barrister and company director, as National Liberal candidate. Leah recalled that it later became known that Furness Withy, the shipbuilders, were prepared to put a ship "on the stocks" if Stephen Furness was adopted. It must have been an offer that couldn't be refused!

It was obvious to Leah and Johnny Pritt that they would have considerable difficulty in winning without the expected Liberal support. John Pritt resigned as prospective candidate and returned to London to become M.P. for Hammersmith. Transport House then drafted in Doctor George Catlin- husband of Vera Brittain and father to Shirley Williams -to join Leah as candidates for this two member constituency.

The 1935 General Election took place on the 14th November of that year. Leah and Doctor Catlin were endorsed by the Executive Committee of the Sunderland Labour Party at a meeting on 26th October and adopted at a public meeting on the 4th November. The Labour Party's first achievement was to get the hours of polling extended from 8.00 p.m. to 9.00 p.m. Then it had to raise the £150 deposit - only bank notes were acceptable as election deposits. The candidates duly handed in their nominations and the fight was on. The Conservative candidate, Mr. Samuel Storey, had been President of the Newspaper Society during 1933/34 and was Chairman of Portsmouth and Sunderland Newspapers Limited. This "advantage" showed clearly throughout the campaign.

The local newspaper, the "Sunderland Echo" gave considerable prominence to the speeches, policies and meetings of the National candidates.

From the outset the "Echo" made it abundantly clear where it stood. One of the first major clashes in the campaign arose from the announcement by Lord Runciman. President of the Board of Trade, that Wearside Shipyards, would get 100,000 tons of orders. Labour said it was an election stunt, Lord Runciman said:-

"I have never done such a dirty trick in all my life."

The "Echo" Editorial on 9th November proclaimed:-

"Which do you believe - Socialist ravings or the cold truth of Lord Runciman - the man who ought to know."

On the same day Leah and Doctor Catlin attended the inauguration of Mr.T. Summerbell as the first Labour Mayor of Sunderland. That afternoon they - and all the other candidates - were guests at Roker Park to see Sunderland play Preston North End.

Prior to the election the Ministry of Health had commissioned a Special Inquiry into Health in the Sunderland area. Leah had publicised its findings which suggested that 33% of mothers were suffering from starvation and 28.4% of children were under-nourished. The "Echo" Editorial responded that:-

" . . . Mrs. Manning tends to suggest there is excessive malnutrition in the town. . . she did not quote that 71.6% of the 700 children examined had normal nutrition."

Leah retorted that what she wanted was for 100% of the children to be properly nourished.

The Editor was confident and knowing:-

"There is no real alternative we know, most of the electors know, but the Socialist candidates are not certain because their platform is made of such rotten timber that they dare not give it a heavy thump." It was not until the two days preceding election day that Labour featured in the front page headlines - instead of on pages 3, 5 or 7.

On Tuesday 12th November, the "Echo" brought Labour on to the front page with a banner headline:-

OCT 12 1935 | TO-MORROW'S WEATHER: BRIGHT INTERVALS | LIGHTING-UP TIME TO-MORROW: | 5 P.M.

The Sunderland Echo
and Shipping Gazette

NO. 19,374 | (SIXTY-SECOND YEAR) TELEPHONE: 59261 | TUESDAY, NOVEMBER 12, 1935 | ONE PENNY

SUNDERLAND SOCIALIST CANDIDATES' "RED" ALLIES

"STAR" SPEAKERS AT A COMMUNIST MEETING

Mrs Manning's "United Front" Election Appeal

The story concerned their attendance at a meeting which had apparently been sponsored by the Communist Party.

The Editorial that day achieved new heights of bias:-

"No one who loves his country, who appreciates straight dealing – a vote in the daylight for issues as clear as daylight – can do other than give their votes equally – one to Mr. Storey and the other to Mr. Furness . . . where ever you vote to the National Government candidates."

The paper advised its readers under the headline of "Think Before You Vote;" On Thursday you will be asked to record your vote in the most momentous election in the history of this country. It will decide whether we have a Socialist Government or continue on the present tide of prosperity now beginning to lick our shores under the National Government."

Despite this opposition the Labour candidates were encouraged by a message from the National Executive of the Free Church Council, saying;-

"We wish you success in your Parliamentary Election."

However, the Sunderland Property Owners Association unanimously resolved to recommend all their members to vote for the National Government.

In the days preceding the election even the letters column of the "Echo" suddenly expanded into a flood of anti Labour correspondence – almost all with pseudonyms. These included:-

Pro-bono Publico – Free Churchman – MacDonaldite – Truth – Ex Marine – C.B. – Wearsider – Nemo – True Briton – Free Voter – Anti Socialist – Proof of Pudding – Country Before Party – Voter – Fair Play – Elector – A Simple Catholic.

The election eve edition again featured Labour on the front page–

NO. 19,375 (SIXTY-SECOND YEAR) TELEPHONE: 56261 WEDNESDAY, NOVEMBER 13, 1935

SOCIALIST POSTERS THAT DESECRATE WAR DEAD

PLAY ON APPEAL FOR REMEMBRANCE DAY

'National' Candidates and Restoration of Industries

The Editorial was content to take as its theme – "Why You Should Vote National Tomorrow."– and page 3 reported:-

The Sunderland Echo
and Shipping Gazette

WEDNESDAY, NOVEMBER 13, 1935 THE SUNDERLAND ECHO AND SHIPPING GAZETTE PAGE 3

Enthusiasm for Sunderland "National" Candidates
PEACE ISSUE IN ELECTION EMPHASIZED

Backing for League in Order to Preserve World's Peace

PERILS OF THE SOCIALIST STATE

On election day the Editor gave his final electoral advice in case anyone had failed to get the message in preceding issues:-

"The one thing that is un-pardonable today is that having a vote not to use it. You must perform your duty as a Britisher and exercise your electoral prerogative if you want a stable government whose methods are certain to bring the greatest measure of peace and prosperity to this country of ours during the next five years then VOTE NATIONAL."

However, not only did Leah have a hostile press to spoil her campaign, on election day she discovered that an early morning leaflet delivery had been made - to a large number of Roman Catholic voters attributing to her statements by the novelist Ethel Mannin. Her novels contained passages on sex and love which shocked readers 50 years ago but which today could be found in daily newspapers and magazines. The author of the leaflet - presumably confusing the two ladies, had extracted a rather frank passage from one of her novels and underneath printed the words:-

"Do you want such a woman to represent you at Westminster?"

In her book, Leah says "I knew when I read the pamphlet we would lose and there was nothing I could do about it. I knew that the whole Catholic vote would desert me. What I found particularly wounding was that I had counted on the Catholic vote. Over the years I have supported aid for Catholic school buildings. My views were well known; I had stuck to them throughout the conferences on religious settlements and had been thanked for my stand by the Catholic Bishops".

So with hope gone, Leah worked through the day and endured the subsequent count. In the event she was bottom of the poll; the full result being:-

S. Furness	(National Liberal)	49,001
S. Storey	(Con)	48,760
Dr. Catlin	(Lab)	32,483
Mrs. L. Manning (Lab)		32,059
Majority		16,518
Percentage poll		78.87% compared to
		81% in 1931.

The Editor of the "Echo" could not disguise his delight and on 16th November rounded off the election campaign with the following words;-

"The people of Sunderland have, as we urged, done their duty by themselves, secondly by the town and thirdly by the country in returning the National candidates . . .it is a magnificent victory, showing clearly that whatever the sufferings of the town may be due to lack of industrial activity the people have faith in the National Government. . . the people of the town have seen so much that is good done by the National Government for peace, disarmament, in Social Services, in creating employment and trade in every direction, in fact - that they refused to be stampeded or scared into putting in Socialists who could not have carried out half the things they promised to do".

Neither Leah - nor anyone else, knew at that time that because of the Second World War the 1935 Members of Parliament would sit until 1945 - and that the people of Sunderland would then reverse the result and give Labour both seats!

F. Willey	(Lab)	38,769
R. Ewart	(Lab)	36,711
S. Furness	(Con)	29,366
S. Storey	(Con)	28,579
T. Tichardson	(Comm)	4,501

Leah was very disappointed with the result and thought she could not again be a successful candidate. She declined to be re-adopted by Sunderland and took her name off of the Labour Party Parliamentary Panel.

Meanwhile in the Epping constituency in 1935 Winston S.Churchill had scored an overwhelming victory and Labour were also bottom of the poll.

Rt. Hon. W. Churchill (National Conservative)	34,849
G. Sharp (Lib)	14,430
J. Ranger (Lab)	9,759
Majority	20,419

Leah could not have foreseen that less than ten years later she would reverse the result in the Epping constituency and become a Member of the most radical British Parliament yet elected.

Leah returned to her work with the National Union of Teachers which involved her in a great deal of travelling around the country. As the clouds of war began to gather over Europe she, like most of her contemporaries on the political left, became more deeply involved in opposing the spread of Fascism.

CHAPTER FIVE
CAMPAIGNING AGAINST FASCISM

At this period of her life, the former M.P. for Islington East was increasingly concerned about the growth of Fascism in Europe and became involved in several organisations which had left-wing and Communist supporters. She joined the Left Book Club and became Joint Secretary of the Co-ordinating Committee against War and Fascism with John Strachey – then a leading advocate of a popular front against Fascism. She also worked for and spoke at meetings of the Committee for the Relief of the Victims of Fascism.

She went to Ridley Road in Hackney to protest against Oswald Mosley in the company of George and Santo Jeger – two brothers both destined to become Labour M.P.'s. In 1934 she visited Spain after the uprising of the Asturias miners and bitterly criticised the repression in the book she wrote, "What I Saw in Spain." She went on a visit to the Soviet Union. Although she never felt motivated even to consider joining the Communist party, she came under increasing suspicion in more orthodox circles in the N.U.T. and the Labour Party alike. Herbert Morrison apparently warned the N.U.T. General Secretary, Sir Frederick Mander, about her and the latter attempted to find out if she was a Communist Party member. His efforts were in vain. Harry Pollitt the Party Secretary, told him:-

"We much admire Leah – but this is a disciplined movement and Leah is a complete individualist."

In 1936, the Spanish Army attempted to seize power and overthrow the democratically elected Government. This precipitated the Spanish Civil War. Leah threw herself into the fray on the side of the Republicans. In the early years of the struggle she visited Spain, and on her return to London she went to the House of Commons, saw Clement Attlee and lobbied others in support of the Republican cause.

In the autumn of 1936 moves were made to bring together the organisations involved in relief work. At a meeting on 6th January 1937 at the House of Commons, 15 organisations came together to formally launch the National

Joint Committee for Spanish Relief. Katherine Marjory, Duchess of Atholl and Conservative M.P. for Kinross and West Perth became Chairman and other prominent members included Ellen Wilkinson Labour M.P. for Jarrow, Wilfred Roberts, Liberal M.P. for North Cumberland, Eleanor Rathbone Independent M.P. for Combined English Universities, Isobel Brown and Leah.

The Duchess, Eleanor Rathbone, Ellen Wilkinson and Dame Rachael Crowdy visited Spain in April and met Dolores Ibarruri, [la Pasionaria] one of the most beloved of the leaders for Spanish democracy. She was born on 9th December 1895. In 1920 she was a founder member of the Spanish Communist Party. She became a member of the Cortes in February 1936. When the civil war ended she fled to Russia and her son was killed at Stalingrad, whilst serving in the Russian army. In 1942 she became General Secretary of the Spanish Communist Party - and President in 1960. After the civil war the Central Committee of the Spanish Communist Party met in secret until 1976 when its first public meeting took place in Rome. She was allowed to return to Spain in 1977 and the following year, at the age of 83, was re-elected to the Cortes. The same year she chaired the IXth Congress of the Spanish Communist Party in Madrid. She died on 12th November 1989.

On her return the Duchess broadcast an appeal for help on behalf of the children of Madrid. She wrote a book on the situation called "Searchlight on Spain" which sold 100,000 copies in a week. She began to be known as 'The Red Duchess' and in July the Spectator commented that there had been "nothing in recent Parliamentary history to compare with the evolution of the Duchess." In April 1938 the Conservative whip was withdrawn from her and in November of that year she was disowned by her Constituency and sought the Chiltern Hundreds.

On 31st July 1936 a meeting at the National Trade Union Club at 24, New Oxford Street, promoted largely on the initiative of Isobel Brown of the Communist Party, set up the Spanish Medical Aid Committee (Fig F. Page 47). Leah became Honorary Secretary until George Jeger was taken on as full-time, paid official. She worked consistently to help raise money which was used to send a regular supply of medical equipment and drugs to the beleaguered country, together with nurses, doctors and other helpers.
The Medical Aid Committee had responsibilities in south and central Spain and in particular for a hospital at Ucles, a village off the Madrid-Valencia Road near Tarancon. Leah had suggested that this hospital be staffed by Spaniards for Spanish wounded only and in August 1937 Dr.Hyacinth

Morgan of S.M.A.C. and T.U.C. went to Madrid to consult the Ministry of Health. They agreed that S.M.A.C. should finance and support a 500 bed base hospital – including provision of a bacteriological laboratory. The hospital was housed in a former monastery at Ucles and within weeks had 800 patients. A shortage of beds was eased when the London Committee was able to buy and send fully equipped ones for £10 each. Many local support groups were formed and Leah spoke at numerous public meetings during 1937 and 1938.

In April 1937 Leah was asked by the Basque delegation in London to go to Bilbao, which was threatened by Franco's forces, and seek to arrange the evacuation of children from the war zone to Britain. She and Edith Pye, of the Society of Friends, made the hazardous journey to the northern Spanish city. They arrived in Spain on 24th April. Two days later Guernica was destroyed and Leah visited the town after the bombing to see the death and destruction. They visited the British Consul, contacted the Basque Government, broadcast over the radio to re-assure the families of those to be evacuated and personally supervised the embarkation of thousands of people. She was in some personal danger and was given permission to carry arms. [Plate 29]. When the British Government, which had agreed to accept some refugees, resisted the despatch of more, she sent telegrams to the Archbishops of Canterbury and Westminster, to Lloyd George and Sir Walter Citrine begging them to intercede.

At 6.40 a.m. on Friday 21st May 1937 the S.S. Habana [Plate 30] left Bilbao with over 3,800 children on board, with 95 maestras (women teachers), 120 Senoritas as helpers and 15 priests. The ship was escorted by the destroyer H.M.S. Forester. Two days later, after a terrible journey, they were welcomed at Southampton by the Duchess of Atholl, Sir Walter and Lady Layton and Sir Walter and Lady Citrine. Many famous names including Cadburys, Horlicks, Rowntrees, Marmite, Jaegers, Co-op, Woolworths, Standard Fireworks, Prudential Assurance, Sidney Bernstein, the R.S.P.C.A. and Marks & Spencer donated goods or money to the relief agencies. In Britain, she helped to organise accommodation. In this, the London Teachers' Association (N.U.T.) was particularly helpful and sent some of the evacuees [Plate 32] to a house in Piercing Hill, Theydon Bois, which for a time was known as the Leah Manning Home. The property, Woodberry, [Plates 31]is now part of Wansfell College. The Salvation Army also did sterling service in helping to house the children from Spain. An exhibition of pictures by Spanish children entitled "Spain – The Child and The War" was held in Central London and Leah wrote the preface to the exhibition guide. She said she had, by a miracle, become the "accidental" mother to 4,000 of them - which gave her a mother's right to speak on their behalf. She described the 118 drawings as representing the children's work, play, joys and sorrows.

Leah was given charge of a group of orphans of Socialist families who were accommodated in Cambridge. The Cambridge Appeal Committee was launched by Canon Craven and historian J.H. Plumb.

The following month a rally was held at the Albert Hall -supported, amongst others by the Duchess of Atholl, Picasso, J.B.S. Haldane, P.M.S. Blackett, H.G. Wells, E.M. Forster, Virginia Woolf, Havelock Ellis, Sean O'Casey, Philip Noel Baker and Dame Sybil Thorndike - with songs by Paul Robeson, raised £11,000 for the emergency appeal.

Leah was soon back in the Spanish Republic. [Plate 33] In July she visited Barcelona, Lamers and Mataro Hospital and the XVth Army Corps Medical Services transport garage and workshop at Alio near Valls.

On 28th July 1938 she visited a front line hospital which was housed in a huge cave. She nursed Harry Dobson for some fourteen hours before he died. Harry, an active member of the Blaenclydach Lodge of the National Union of Mineworkers, had first met Leah when she addressed an anti-fascist rally in South Wales. He had been imprisoned following an anti-fascist rally in Tonypandy. On the day of his release he volunteered for service in Spain. He became a member of the XVth Brigade and was seriously wounded in fighting at Ebro. She tells how he briefly regained consciousness after an emergency operation and "stared hard at me for a minute or two and then said - why surely it is comrade Leah Manning". After his death she wrote to his sister Mrs Razey.

Jim Fyrth in his book, *"The Signal That Was Spain"* quotes Leah's description of the occasion:-

"It was a fantastic night, as I sat by this dying comrade, passing along the high winding road on the side opposite the cave, hundreds of camions (trucks) passed by with singing reserves and loads of material and ammunition on their way to Ebro, whilst winding down the glen at the bottom came the ambulances with the dead, dying and wounded men."

On her return she once more spoke at meetings throughout the country in the Republican cause and continued to do so as long as the struggle continued. Her interest in Spain never disappeared and later, when M.P. for Epping, she spoke on various aspects of the subject and strongly opposed the resumption of diplomatic relations. In 1947 she undertook a lecture tour of America at the invitation of the Abraham Lincoln Battalion (part of the

International Brigades), to raise money for orphanages in France and Belgium which still had Spanish refugee children.

Her experiences posed for her the question of the validity of pacifism. In 1935 she campaigned strongly in support of the Peace Ballot organised by the League of Nations Union. This showed that while a majority of people were for an all-round reduction in armaments, most people believed in armed resistance to aggression. After considerable soul-searching, she came down in favour of re-armament as a shield against Fascism. She states in her autobiography that she had already come to this position by the time that she stood for Sunderland in the 1935 General Election. The Spanish Civil War strengthened her view on this issue and in 1938 she was strongly opposed to the Munich Agreement which the British Prime Minister, Neville Chamberlain, made with Adolf Hitler, accepting a dismemberment of Czechoslovakia. After Munich Leah considered that another war was inevitable. She joined the London Ambulance Service and spent evenings and nights driving various ambulance vehicles around East London from their base under the railway arches at Bethnal Green.

When war came in September 1939 she was coldly critical of the opposition of the Communist Party and subsequently of the Russian invasion of Finland. Leah was still Assistant Education Officer of the N.U.T. when the Union decided to evacuate its headquarters to Toddington Manor in Gloucestershire. Initially she declined to go but, after Will had been sent to work in Canada, it was financially necessary to have a job. She rejoined the N.U.T. staff and became evacuation liaison officer - travelling to every evacuation area in the country. She still found the opportunity to visit wartime London and whenever possible went to the mid-day concerts by Myra Hess, at the National Gallery. Her flat at Red Lion Square suffered bomb damage and in escaping she injured a knee. Later in the war Leah became Head of Organisation at the N.U.T.'s London office at Hamilton House. She had a heavy burden of administrative responsibilities and was involved in some preparatory work for the 1944 Education Bill.

As previously in her life, she combined this with outside political work. Once Russia entered the war, she was prominent in the Aid to Russia Organisation and became a spokeswoman for the "Second Front Now" campaign in favour of opening a second front against Nazi occupied Europe. As the tide turned against Hitler, her admiration for Churchill was tempered by her opposition to his support for the conservative forces in Italy and Greece once the Germans had been forced to leave. More and more her thoughts turned to the issues of the post-war world, and her desire to get back into the political struggle, as of old, grew more and more powerful. Early in 1945, returning from a weekend in Cambridge, she motored through Epping and said to her passenger that in a few weeks time Churchill's bland smile would beam from every house and hoarding. She then had no idea of what Epping would come to mean to her.

CHAPTER SIX
THE 1945 GENERAL ELECTION

Early in 1945, she went to the Labour Party's Headquarters at Transport House, to ask about the possibility of being selected once again as a candidate for Parliament. At the age of 59 her ambitions had mellowed and she indicated that she would be willing to fight a seat in which the chance of election was remote. The National Agent, Frank Shepherd, suggested Epping, from which a request for a candidate had just been received. Having been re-assured that this was no longer Winston Churchill's constituency, but a new division created by re-distribution, Leah agreed to go forward for selection.

The area, which had been divided from the former Epping seat, consisted of Chingford, Waltham Abbey, Epping, Harlow and the parishes of North Weald, Magdalen Laver, Sheering, Matching, Latton, Netteswell, Great and Little Parndon, Epping Upland, Roydon and Nazeing. It was traditionally Conservative but the war had resulted in numerous evacuees moving into the area and there was some evidence of a wind of change within some of the older communities.

The newly formed Epping Constituency Labour Party held its selection conference at 107, Hall Lane, Chingford [Plate 34].on the 8th June 1945. Leon Maclaren, the prospective candidate for the old Division, was invited but did not attend. This left two valid nominations T.J.R. Langmead and Leah Manning, the latter being selected by 10 votes to 3. Her Nomination Paper was subsequently completed as follows:-

Proposer Mrs. L. Oakes, Seconder Mr. E. Lacey and

Mr. P. Stammers,	Mr. A.E. Pettifer,
Mr. W.J. Buckley,	Mr. R.C. Lacey,
Mrs. E. Crampin,	Mr. A. Gibson,
Mr. D.J. Solomons,	Mr. E. Crampin.

Chingford Councillor George Smith was appointed Agent with Colin

Douglas Sub-Agent for Harlow and Ted Woodland Trustee of the Campaign Fund. She had two opponents Colonel A.R.Wise M.B.E. T.D., who had been the Tory MP for Smethwick since 1931. He had decided to leave that Division after disagreement with the local Association. He was Chairman of Aeroplane and Motor Aluminium Castings Limited., and, for the Liberals, Sir Sydney Robinson J.P. from Snaresbrook. He had been selected as an Alderman on the Essex County Council, was a Freeman of the City of London and knew the Harlow District well. His building company, Sydney Robinson Limited, had built a pre-war Council estate at Potter Street. He had sat as Liberal M.P. for Chelmsford from 1923/24.

Leah issued a radical election address with the headline:-

THE PEOPLE WON THE WAR, NOW LET THEM WIN THE PEACE, VOTE LABOUR

It read:-

"I have had the honour of being selected as the Labour Candidate for the Epping Division, at the forthcoming Parliamentary Election, and I wish to place before you the policy for which I stand. This Election is probably the most important in British history. It follows a massive struggle in Europe; a struggle which has been crowned with victory because the whole resources of the nation have been mobilised to that end. Now we have to consider, as a nation, the best way in which our resources should be mobilised for peace.

After Victory.

While victory in Europe is assured for the United Nations, the British Labour Party is firmly resolved that Japanese barbarism shall be defeated just as decisively as Nazi aggression and tyranny. These victories must not be ascribed to any one man. They will be the reward and the justification for the sacrifices of millions of our people everywhere. The men and women in the Services, the factories and Civil Defence; those who have toiled unceasingly on the land to get our food and those who have faced tremendous hazards to bring it across the seas; the housewife in the home, and the children and their teachers in the evacuation areas - the glory of victory belongs to them all.

These men and women and their families deserve and will expect something very different from the shabby treatment meted out to the generation that "won the war to end war".

The National Interests First.

The nation wants food, work and homes. It wants a high standard of health and of education so that every boy and girl shall be given the chance to develop the best that is in them. Our old folks want to be sure that after a life of service to the community their old age is not to be fraught with anxiety and shadowed by poverty. Labour accepts the Nation's challenge. These are civilised human needs and must be met. You must not be astonished to find that candidates other than those representing the Labour Party put forward a similar programme. But the test of a political programme is whether it is sufficiently in earnest about its objectivess to adopt the means needed to realise them. This is where the Labour Party differs radically from the other parties. It puts the nation before any section. It will not be deterred from the tasks it sets out to achieve by the claims of those vested interests which have never felt any responsibility for the nation as a whole, and have always stood in the way of its full prosperity.

Whilst no -one would wish to carry over into the days of peace all the features of war- time organisation, I am convinced that it will be quite impossible to carry out the great programme of peace-time reconstruction which the Nation is demanding, unless industry, the public utility services and the great financial institutions are harnessed to the public interest. These are the controls Labour is determined to continue if it secures victory at the polls. The Tories would like the Government and Parliament to stand aside so that the monopolist and private interests may do as they please. This is exactly what happened at the end of the last war.

Will History Repeat Itself?

Yes it will, unless you use your vote with judgment and care, and a lively remembrance of what life was like in this country between the two wars. For eighteen of those twenty-one years the Tories were in power with overwhelming majorities. Let me remind you of one or two things. Farming, which during the war period had been on top of the world, sank back into terrible depression. Farmers went bankrupt, agricultural workers lost their wage standards, the houses which had been promised to the rural areas never materialised. After one or two short booms in industry there were long and terrible periods of slump, when millions of our fellow countrymen were unemployed, eating out their hearts on the dole. At the behest of international capital cuts were made in the social services, wages and salaries were driven down, and to the iniquity of the cut in unemployment pay was added the blacker iniquity of the means test. These miseries were the direct result of the Tory victories in the khaki election of 1918. Then, as now, they shouted hysterically "Away with controls". Believe me, the Tories have nothing to offer you. In this half of the twentieth century they have staggered and stumbled from peace and unemployment, into war and jobs for all, and back again into peace and unemployment. You should say "NEVER AGAIN".

Let Us Build A Real Peace.

If social progress is to proceed without these violent setbacks, Britain must help the world towards international security and prosperity. As long as some nations are poverty stricken and open to exploitation, so long will there be friction and violent economic rivalries leading to war. We must take our place in a strong World Security Organisation which will actively protect the peace of the world, by mediation and arbitration if possible, but also by having at its disposal an international armed force which will make the prohibition of war effective. In the case of Germany and Japan, the United Nations must prevent any attempt at re-armament on the part of these two aggressive powers, and by the re-establishment of a Republican Government in Spain, must root out the last remnants of Fascism in Europe. Above all, remembering that "peace is indivisible", we must allow no misundersandings to corrupt our friendship with our two great allies, the U.S.A. and the U.S.S.R.

To All Men And Women In The Forces.

The gallantry and devotion you have displayed, in your titanic struggle to preserve the liberties of our country, deserve well of the nation. I pledge myself if returned as your Member, to see that there is no vital change made in the demobilisation plans so carefully worked out by Mr.Bevin; that every assistance shall be given you to reinstate yourself in civil life and to train for a career, if that is necessary, and that the economic and industrial arrangements of this country shall be such, that you will not be thrown on the industrial scrapheap as were so many of the generation that won the last war. Your future well-being and that of your fellow-citizens is bound up with the return of a powerful Labour majority at the General Election." Her principal policies were emphasised under the heading - "What I Stand For."

What I Stand For

The complete defeat of Japan.

A World Security Organisation to keep the peace.

Jobs for all by keeping up the people's purchasing power through good wages, family allowances and pensions, and through the planned direction of investment by a National Investment Board.

The public ownership of the Bank of England and key industries of coal, transport, and iron and steel.

Strict public supervision of monopolies and cartels.

A prosperous agricultural industry to give a fair return to farmers and farm workers, and to produce more and better food at reasonable prices.

A housing drive until every family has a well-built and comfortable home.

The best education to give all children a fair start in life.

A National Health Service to protect the people's health, and early legislation extending Social Security to all.

In her heart, the candidate did not expect to win, but when the General Election came she was delighted to find her public meetings packed with enthusiastic supporters. The Central Committee Rooms were established in the Co-op Hall at Epping and others at Forest Drive, Theydon Bois, Churchgate Street, Harlow and at Chingford. Public meetings held included 21st June at Roydon Village Hall, 25th June at the Congregational Hall Nazeing, and the Crown Hotel, Old Nazeing, on 28th June at St. John's Hall Epping, the next night at the Queens Rooms, North Weald, at Theydon Bois School on 2nd July and then the Victoria Hall at Harlow on 3rd July. A crowded eve of poll meeting took place at the British Restaurant at Epping on 4th July, where unfortunately Leah injured her ankle in a fall. By the end of the campaign Leah was certain that Labour could win and said that the best reward for Churchill would be an honourable retirement.

On polling day, 5th July 1945, it rained during the morning but brightened later. The polling appeared heavy to observers but because of the delay in receiving service votes no results were declared until 26th July.

At the close of the poll Leah said:-

"I should say I am in - we had a very heavy poll which is always best for us - on my tour of the constituency I found that the Labour Party organisation was the best of the three and the only one to use polling cards." On the following day Colonel Wise said:- "I think I stand a good chance." Sir Sydney Robinson was not hopeful and said he had lacked party workers.

On 7th July the West Essex Gazette headlined its election report EPPING – LABOUR? It said it had been a very open fight. Sir Sydney Robinson had not made much headway with his Liberal candidature and support for him had been disappointing. But the reporter, C.E. Waller, suggested that every vote cast for Robinson was one less for the Tory man Lieutenant Colonel Wise. He noted that over 40% of the electorate was in Chingford of which the South was firmly Labour and the North firmly Conservative. He thought that some of the villages would also be Labour but that overall it would be a very close thing indeed. Noting however that on balance, most service votes were likely to go to Labour, he said that his bet was on Leah Manning.

At the election count on 26th July, Leah was in attendance early wearing a fur cape over her navy blue dress. Colonel Wise arrived at 11.10 a.m. in a brown suit with a grey trilby and smoking a pipe. Leah greeted him with a handshake and said, "Well, Colonel Wise, we are running neck and neck if not nose to nose." The excitement in the count, at Epping Armoury, climaxed at 11.38 a.m. when the Deputy Returning Officer declared the result that made Leah the first M.P. for the new constituency of Epping – and the first and only woman to have held the seat. In the event the Forces' vote and influence had carried the field.

Leah Manning (Lab)	15993
Lt. Colonel A.R. Wise (Con)	15006
Sir Sydney Robinson (Lib)	5314
Majority 987.	

72% of the registered electorate voted.

This compared to the 1935 result in the old Epping Constituency which was much larger and included Woodford, Loughton and Chigwell. This was:-

Rt. Hon. W. Churchill (Con)	34849
G. Sharp (Lib)	14430
J. Ranger (Lab)	9758
Majority	20419

(J. Ranger won the Ilford South seat for Labour in 1945.)

Leah gave thanks to the Presiding Officer and staff and thanked those who had voted for her – as well as those who had not. "I will represent you all", she said, "This magnificent victory is due to the belief among people that it is in the Socialist and Labour hands that the future welfare of the people of this country and the world depends. Our victory is due to the spirit of unity among people who believed in a progressive cause." She paid tribute to the splendid teamwork and the efforts of the campaign committee and other workers.

The victory was greeted with elation by the Labour supporters. An Epping farmworker, Chris Morris, and his bell-ringing associates rang the church bells; the streets were agog with excitement and, in remote fields, pea pickers and land workers cheered when they heard the news. Traditional Conservative voters were stunned. As Labour swept to power, Winston Churchill resigned with regret that he had not been permitted to complete the war against Japan. However, he said, "All plans and preparations have been made." Then, in an apparent reference to the top secret plan for the forthcoming atomic attack on Japan he said "The result may come much quicker than we have hitherto been entitled to expect. "

Within days –on 6th August 1945, 160,000 men, women and children were killed or injured as the City of Hiroshima was destroyed in an atomic flash and the world entered the nuclear age.

At Westminster, Leah resolved to be a good backbench M.P. rather than to seek advancement as a P.P.S. to a Minister. She won acclaim as a champion of women's causes and as an outstanding constituency M.P. She visited every corner of her constituency and, regardless of politics, whosoever approached her was given devoted attention. Housing, pensions, war damage, re-building, drainage, flooding, rationing, education, the needs of agriculture, industry, all varieties of personal problems fell within her sphere. She rapidly became a household name and new local Labour Parties were formed where they had never existed before.

CHAPTER SEVEN
THE HOUSE OF COMMONS 1945 - 1950

In the House of Commons,[Plates 35-37] the new M.P. for Epping specialised in education, foreign affairs, agriculture and women's issues. The local issues were not overlooked and these ranged from sanitation at Lower Nazeing School, to the repair of thatched cottages, deficiencies in local bus and train services, flooding at Dobbs Weir, war damage claims in Epping and the shortage of baby napkins in Epping, Harlow and Bishop's Stortford.

On entry to the House she would always hang her coat on the "men's" hooks, continuing the campaign against discrimination in the House that she had started with her visit in 1930.

Her first contribution in the new parliament was on 17th August 1945 in the Debate on the King's speech. Leah said:-

"Speaking as a Member, who has been exiled from this place for sometime, I would say that I have returned with none of those desperate feelings with which the right Hon. Gentleman the member for Saffron Walden (Mr. Butler) expected us to return. . . I do not feel at all like the morning after the night before. Indeed I am experiencing a very great deal of exhilaration in seeing what the Gracious speech outlines - a programme which I and many other members on this side of the House have spent our whole lives in trying to bring before the electorate of this country. Most of us realise that this is the only way to bring happiness and security to this country. . . there is no question that interests me more than the nationalisation of our water supply. Not only does every decent civilisation depend upon a plentiful supply of pure water, but the health of our farming industry, and agriculture generally, also depend on this."

She went on to urge a co-ordinated drive on housing provision . . . "I remember that in one of his more lucid broadcasts, the Right Hon. Member for Woodford (Winston Churchill) exhorted the women of this country to multiply and be fruitful. Many women would be only too willing to do that if they could get back their husbands and sweethearts from the forces and were given homes . . . it has been a great pleasure to me to come back to the

House and find on the first occasion that here is a King's speech to which I can give my wholehearted assent and hope it will be passed speedily into law."

The new Government was determined to establish a National Health Service, and a National Insurance Scheme, plus a whole range of welfare benefits. It put up pensions and introduced the Industrial Injuries Act to provide proper compensation for people injured at work. It launched a major housing drive to provide good homes for all. It built schools, abolished grammar school fees, opened the doors of the universities to many previously debarred. It took the coal mines, electricity, gas, road, rail and air transport, Cable and Wireless and the Bank of England into public ownership, making their products and services available for all. In the Epping Constituency, as elsewhere, electricity, gas and main drainage were provided to many who had never before had access to them. As the men and women were demobilised, they easily found jobs and unemployment appeared to be a thing of the past. As house building grew, living standards rose at a steady pace.

In 1947 when the "New Look" longer skirts became fashionable she and Bessie Braddock, a Liverpool M.P., whose size matched Leah's, campaigned for additional clothing coupons. In reply to a question to the President of the Board of Trade (Harold Wilson) she was told that Princess Elizabeth had been allocated 23 coupons for her wedding and the bridesmaids and pages 10 each.

Leah Manning was not, however, mere voting fodder. In December 1948 her and 50 others voted against increasing National Service from twelve to eighteen months. In March of that year during a debate on Civil Defence she said:-

"The Iron Curtain which we are told exists between East and West has today given place to a kind of sheet in a shadow play across which both sides see a phantasmagoria of distorted, horrible, grotesque people passing. Someone has to tear down the sheet and show people on both sides that we are ordinary human beings hating war and longing for peace. Unless the Government can do that, the Government have failed in all they set out to do."

In the House she raised her voice whenever she felt she had a contribution to make. Thus she pressed for a Family Planning Service as part of the National Health Service - an aim only realised many years later. She supported the Bill which sought to provide analgesia free to women having children and incurred official displeasure since it was sponsored by a Conservative - Peter (later Lord) Thorneycroft.

Throughout the 1945-1950 Parliaments she maintained a strong interest in educational matters which form the largest section of the Parliamentary Index (beginning on Page 95). She supported the party and Government policy of abolishing the eleven plus exam and thought that purpose built comprehensives could hardly be bettered.

In February 1948, 40 years on from the privations of her first teaching post in Cambridge, Leah must have been pleased - and proud, to edit a Labour Party pamphlet entitled "Growing Up - Labour's plan for Women and Children". It was aimed at recruiting members of Women's Sections and it detailed party policies and plans for women and children. Pregnant mothers could obtain a grey ration book which offered priority on a wide range of foods and 70 supplementary clothing coupons for the baby's layette. Extra food included 1 packet of dried egg - free of points -every 8 weeks, 1 additional egg at each allocation, extra meat ration, concentrated orange juice at 5d for a 6 oz bottle and a free packet - every 6 weeks - of chocolate coated vitamin A and D tablets or alternatively Cod Liver Oil.

Pregnant mothers with low incomes were able to get an extra pint of milk a day for a penny halfpenny and everyone had the right to extra milk for 30 weeks after confinement. The pamphlet also included details about arrangements for confinement, home helps and Post Natal care.

Leah restated the Party's commitment to Day Nurseries and Nursery Schools for all children and said that every infant school should have a nursery wing for 3-5 year olds - staffed by trained and qualified nursery teachers and nurses. 40 years on from her 1908 campaigning in Cambridge,she noted that since school milk had become free, the take-up had increased from 72% to 92% and that since 1945 some 4,000 school canteens had been provided with another 1,000 in course of provision. She pledged that the extension of the school meals service would continue until it was universally available. She re-affirmed the principle that the nation should help in the maintainance of its children by universally available family allowances and noted that over four million children benefitted in the first year of the scheme.

She said the Government were now investing more wealth and thought into future citizens of Britain than had ever been known in its history. A tremendous amount was being done for the health and general welfare of mothers and children was in accordance with the extremely high standard of social legislation for which the British Labour Government had become world famous. She concluded that, "Future generations of Britain will prove the wisdom of this great new development towards social justice and to democracy."

Later that year she said:-

"Somehow we women must take a hand and show that we can run things better. For centuries men have had it their way and look what has happened. War after war. Finally if we can't make the men see reason we'll have to copy Lysistrata – but I'm sure men would never let it go as far as that."

She could also be vitriolic to the opposition and once said:-

"I have been a teacher for very many years, and I have taught mentally defective children. Quite honestly, I did not find it nearly as difficult to make them understand as I and my Hon. Friends on this side of the House, find it to make Hon. Members oppposite understand what was said."

On another occasion, at a Labour Party rally at Weymouth, she said of the local Member, Viscount Hinchingbrooke:-

"I always listen to the noble Lord when he speaks in the House. His speeches are compounded of 10% good honest common sense and 90% absolute and complete nonsense."

Neither was she always kind to her comrades. In 1947, expressing annoyance at delay in obtaining information about Women Teachers' salaries she said curtly:-

"If I give my Right Hon. Friend a very long time – say until the crisis is over – does he think he could find out.?"

This led Major Tufton Beamish (Lewes) to retort:-

"Is the Hon. Lady for Epping an example of a woman teacher "at the maximum?"

She was also a very influential figure in the Epping Constituency Labour Party. At its meetings, at Epping Co-op Hall, she would sit at the top table and issue instructions to the Chairman, Secretary or anyone else on the conduct or business of the meeting.

On International Women's Day on 9th March 1946 [Plate 38] she chaired an international conference at Beaver Hall, London, with representatives from all parts of the world. On the 1948 Day, Leah appeared as the prisoner in an "Equal Pay Trial", [Plate 39] again at Beaver Hall, London, with D.N. Pritt acting as Presiding Judge and John Platt Mills as the Defending Counsel. The "Trial" was arranged by the National Committee for the Celebration of International Women's Day. (Twenty-two years later, in 1970, the Equal Pay Act was passed – it came into operation in 1975). Later that year Leah was U.K. delegate to the Second Annual Conference of the World Movement for World Federal Government. [Plate 40] The Conference considered a proposal for a "People's Convention", whose members would be elected by the people of the world – one member per million voters.

Leah also had a less serious side. The same year she had met Sophie Tucker and told her that because of her size and weight she was known as the Sophie Tucker of Westminster. Indeed Leah sang some of Sophie's songs at parties. She often claimed to be a bad driver - and therefore the best customer of the Co-op Service Station at Potter Street, Harlow.

In the House of Commons, one proposal particularly concerned her and her Constituency: the New Towns Bill of 1946, introduced by Lewis (later Lord) Silkin. Leah served on the Commons Committee considering the Bill. It proposed the designation of a number of New Towns around London for the re-housing of Londoners and one of the sites chosen was at Harlow. [Plate 41] When the news broke, some of the older residents, but above all the more affluent, formed the Harlow Defence Association, with the explicit task of opposing the proposed development. A number of Leah's supporters, on the other hand, arranged meetings and launched a petition in favour of the building of a New Town at Harlow. Outstanding among these were Ted Woodland, Alf Brown, Fred James and Bill Fisher - all dedicated Labour Party members and Parish Councillors in the new designated area. An enquiry was held and a petition containing the signatures of hundreds of residents supporting the development was sent to Lewis Silkin by Ted Woodland as Chairman of the Netteswell Parish Council. This demonstration of public support was vital in helping to ensure that the New Town was built and Leah was thrilled with the decision to go ahead, for which she consistently campaigned.

Indeed one of the highlights of Leah's Parliamentary career was on 5th July 1946 in the final debate on the New Towns Bill when she addressed the House of Commons thus:-

"We have now come to the concluding stages of a Bill which I think we shall all look back upon in the future as marking a great turning point, in the housing and population of this country. I have listened with mounting horror to the remarks of the noble Lord the member of South Dorset (Viscount Hinchingbrooke) - horror not only at what he said today, but because I feel that in the mind of the noble Lord, there must be a tremendous conflict going on all the time. I remember a speech he made not so long ago upon which I congratulated him in the Lobby. It was a progressive, forward-looking speech. This morning he makes a speech which is fraught with the gravest reaction that we have heard, even from those benches, for months. I will tell the noble Lord what this Bill will do when it becomes law. It will place in the hands of simple, honest, decent, kindly folk a key, opening to them a design of gracious living, that gracious living which he and his class have enjoyed for many centuries, but we and our class, the class to which he referred, have never enjoyed. It is true, as he says, that we have risen today from the damage which was done to our class in the 19th Century. We have done so by continually fighting; and now we have risen above it we say, "we must make something better for our children and our grandchildren," and that is one of the things which this Bill sets out to do. Far from the Bill emerging unimproved from the Committee stage we find that owing to the extreme courtesy, patience and helpfulness of the Ministers concerned, it has emerged a much better Bill. It is now a Bill of which anybody may be proud.

It is not, as the noble Lord said with such terrible fatalism, a dead letter before it has reached the Statute Book, or a Bill which cannot possibly be put into operation. As soon as it is an Act I hope that we shall begin to put in operation the design which those of us who have framed this Bill will have in mind.

I have a special interest in this Bill, because in the constituency which I represent, I hope - indeed, I almost pray - we shall have at one end a new town. At the other end we have a beautiful forest, one of the lungs of the most ugly and depressed parts of London. The alternatives which face the country planners of today are either to build on those green belts and beautiful open spaces or to build new towns. I do not want to see Epping Forest built over. It belongs to the people. We fought for it and we got it for ourselves. I do not want to see Wanstead Flats, the playground of the East End, built over. Half of my constituency is right up against those open spaces and the beautiful forest, the like of which, no doubt, the noble Lord has surrounding the mansion in which he lives. But the people living in those parts of London have not got such places up against their back doors. At their back doors they have broken bricks, broken bottles, rubble and other distressing sights. These open spaces are their only resorts. If the building programme which is necessary is carried out, it means either building on those open spaces or going out into the countryside."

Viscount Hinchingbrooke intervened here and said:-

"I do not want the Hon. Lady to assume that I am opposed to open spaces near large towns. I have not said anything of the sort. Indeed, I am very much in favour of re- planning London to enable the people of whom the Hon. Lady is speaking to enjoy the fullest access to open spaces."

But Leah continued her plea for a New Town at Harlow:-

"The noble Lord cannot have it both ways. He is in a cleft stick. Let me take the Borough of Chingford, which is the biggest part of my constituency. There are 3,000 young people living there who are waiting for houses. We are right up against Walthamstow, a built-up area, at one end, and we are up against Epping Forest at the other end. We have space to build 600 houses for those 3,000 people. I ask the noble Lord where else are those people to go unless the Minister will give us a new town in Harlow or some such place? The noble Lord says, "Remember Stevenage, remember the people who are to be turned out of their farms, their beautiful houses and little shops." Stevenage, as the noble Lord knows, was a "trumped up" affair by people who did not belong to Stevenage, but who were imported into Stevenage, as Hon. Members opposite will import their spies and myrmidons who work for them into almost every conflict which they think is likely to arise, from bread rationing to new towns, and whatever else happens to be a matter of political controversy.

I was a little wise as far as Harlow is concerned. I got in first, before the crowd. What did I find at a crowded meeting held there? I did not find people pleading and crying that they were to be turned out of their shops, their houses and farms, but a great mass of people who looked forward to the day when a new town would arise in this very ill-served town, ill-served educationally, culturally and industrially and in every possible way such as people who live in many small country towns are served.

That does not mean that there are not some points about which even I am anxious so far as the new towns are concerned. I am very anxious about the farming and agricultural interest of those people who live in and around the areas which are to be designated areas. . . indeed my own, poor, remote, small cottage will also be engulfed in this new town, but I do not mind that. I am looking forward to it. I am prepared to give up the serenity of my rural life if it means for a great mass of other people, something better than they have ever known.

Like the noble Lord, I am concerned about the agricultural interest of the people, who have put into their farms much more than work, because the man who farms the land does put into his farm more than work. He puts in his thoughts and his interests, and very often prayers, and sometimes his farm has been in the possession of himself and his family for many years. I believe the Minister has in mind the idea of planning some of these towns as neighbourhood units so that they have their own green belt. On those green belts should be the farms that it will be possible to retain by this form of planning. Those farms can still be used by the people who have lived in them. To give them something else would not be the same thing. In Harlow I can envisage the possibility of a central town - a fairly small town - with those farms around it, and then the smaller towns or neighbourhood units. If my right Hon. Friend would plan this new town in that way it would help us to avoid disturbing something of those agricultural interests for which the noble Lord, like myself, cares so greatly and hope will be preserved. Fortunately, he and I have that view in common.

I welcome more than any other Bill which has been before this House since I have been a Member, this Bill, which has now reached its concluding stage, and that the Minister will have the great pride and the pleasure of seeing not castles in the air, because the Socialist Government have their feet far too firmly on the ground – (Laughter) well, believe me, I should find it very difficult to float in the air. I hope the Minister will have the pleasure of seeing this Bill result in new towns springing up and putting into the hands of many humble people the key to a design for gracious and beautiful living."

Leah could hardly have foreseen that 40 years on the completed new town[Plate 41] would have its own land and housing shortage. Happily she was able to watch the town grow and participate in its industrial, community and political life.

Although the new town proposal did not meet with universal support, on other issues Leah won the approval of her opponents. One of the least sympathetic sections of her electorate, by and large, was that of the farmers. In fact, however, she was a champion of the farmers' interests. She served on the standing committee for the Agricultural Act of Tom Williams which laid the basis for a new deal for farming. She also worked wholeheartedly on behalf of the glasshouse producers represented in the Lea Valley Growers Association.

Membership of the External Affairs Committee and the Empire Parliamentary Union, enabled her to continue an interest in international affairs. In 1947 she Chaired the Women's Committee Against War and Fascism. She spoke against the 1946 American Loan and always regretted that she failed to vote against it as well. She regarded Marshall Aid as an attempt to keep Europe in the American sphere of interest. She became a persistent critic of the foreign policy of Ernest Bevin and she viewed with dismay the development of the Cold War. She rejoiced at the introduction of the Independence of India Bill as an act of outstanding historical importance. She could never forget what she had seen of the war in Spain and Europe as a whole and she had a deep longing for peace and international understanding. Above all she believed in the United Nations and travelled widely in Eastern Europe and the United States to press her objectives.

In 1947 Leah had, after years of denial, been given a visa to go to Spain. She visited a woman teacher who had been sentenced to death, which was

GIVEN AT THE GENERAL REGISTER OFFICE, LONDON

*Application Number. R. 15785

BIRTH in the Sub-district of Droitwich

REGISTRATION DISTRICT Droitwich in the *County of Worcester*

1856

Columns:—									
No.	When and where born	Name, if any	Sex	Name and surname of father	Name, surname and maiden surname of mother	Occupation of father	Signature, description and residence of informant	When registered	Signature of registrar	Name entered after registration
	Fourteenth March 1856 Abberah Park Droitwich	Elizabeth Jane	Girl	Charles Williams Frith	Hannah Margaret Frith formerly Tolppou	Station Foreman Railway	C. W. Frith Father Abberah Park Droitwich	Fourteenth May 1856	John Thomas Morgan Registrar	

CERTIFIED to be a true copy of an entry in the certified copy of a Register of Births in the District above mentioned.
Given at the GENERAL REGISTER OFFICE, LONDON, under the Seal of the said Office, the 2nd day of April 19 86

This certificate is issued in pursuance of the Births and Deaths Registration Act 1953. Section 34 provides that any certified copy of an entry purporting to be sealed or stamped with the seal of the General Register Office shall be received as evidence of the birth or death to which it relates without any further or other proof of the entry, and no certified copy purporting to have been given in the said Office shall be of any force or effect unless it is sealed or stamped as aforesaid.

CAUTION:—It is an offence to falsify a certificate or to make or knowingly use a false certificate or a copy of a false certificate intending it to be accepted as genuine to the prejudice of any person or to possess a certificate knowing it to be false without lawful authority.

Form A502M   Dd 8349844   100M   4/85   Mcr(300230)

BXB   162225

*See note overleaf

1

2

3 Family group showing Leah's father and mother.

4

5

7

6

9

8

10

11

12

13

15

14

17

18

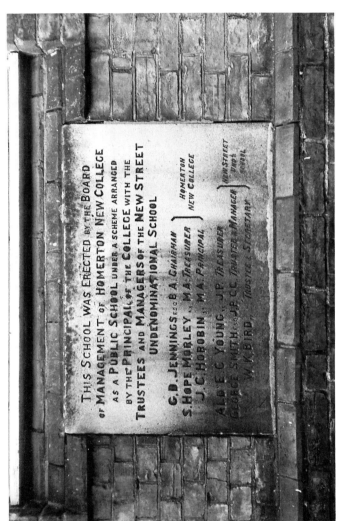

THIS SCHOOL WAS ERECTED BY THE BOARD
OF MANAGEMENT OF HOMERTON NEW COLLEGE
AS A PUBLIC SCHOOL UNDER A SCHEME ARRANGED
BY THE PRINCIPAL OF THE COLLEGE WITH THE
TRUSTEES AND MANAGERS OF THE NEW STREET
UNDENOMINATIONAL SCHOOL

G. B. JENNINGS ESQ B. A. CHAIRMAN ⎫
S. HOPE MORLEY . M. A. TREASURER ⎬ HOMERTON
J. C. HOROBIN . M. A. PRINCIPAL ⎭ NEW COLLEGE

ALD E. C. YOUNG . J. P. TREASURER ⎫ NEW STREET
GEORGE SMITH ESQ J. P. C. E. TRUSTEE & MANAGER ⎬ UND D.
W. K. BIRD, TRUSTEE & SECRETARY ⎭ SCHOOL

19

CERTIFIED COPY OF AN ENTRY OF MARRIAGE

Given at the GENERAL REGISTER OFFICE, LONDON

Application Number..K.II.77244.

Registration District Cambridge

1913. Marriage solemnized at Holy Sepulchre Church

in the Town of Cambridge in the County of Cambridge

No.	(1) When married	(2) Name and Surname	(3) Age	(4) Condition	(5) Rank or profession	(6) Residence at the time of marriage	(7) Father's name and surname	(8) Rank of profession of father
197.	July 26 1913.	William Henry Manning	30	Bachelor	Observatory Assistant	The Observatory Cambridge	Joseph Manning	Market Gardener
		Elizabeth Leah Rencett	29.	Spinster		bridge Street Cambridge.	Charles William Rencett	Timber Merchant

Married in the Parish aforesaid according to the Rites and Ceremonies of the Church of England after Banns by me

This marriage was solemnized between us {
William Henry Manning
Elizabeth Leah Rencett.
}
in the presence of us, {
Edith Tucker
William T.G. Oxtoby J.H Priest
}

CERTIFIED to be a true copy of an entry in the certified copy of a Register of Marriages in the District above mentioned.

Given at the GENERAL REGISTER OFFICE, LONDON, under the Seal of the said Office, the 2nd day of August 19 .

MB 375591

This certificate is issued in pursuance of section 65 of the Marriage Act 1949. Sub-section 3 of that section provides that any certified copy of an entry purporting to be sealed or stamped with the seal of the General Register Office shall be received as evidence of the marriage to which it relates without any further or other proof of the entry, and no certified copy purporting to have been given in the said Office shall be of any force or effect unless it is sealed or stamped as aforesaid.

CAUTION:—It is an offence to falsify a certificate or to make or knowingly use a false certificate or a copy of a false certificate intending it to be accepted as genuine to the prejudice of any person, or to possess a certificate knowing it to be false without lawful authority.

Form A513 Dd 8098259 84/0006 11M. 5/88 Mcr(733887)

20

21

22

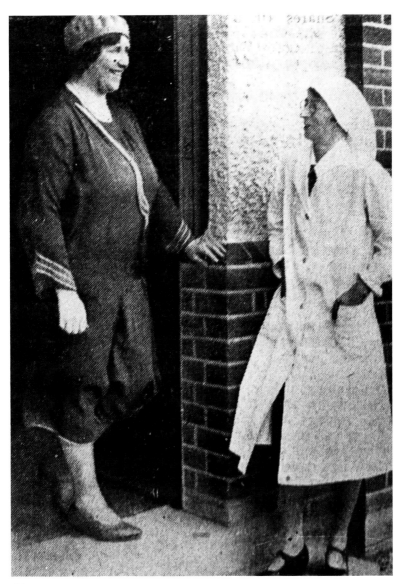

Hearing Their First Case.

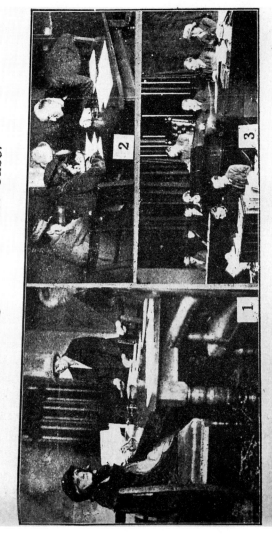

[Chronicle Photos.]

Three of the five lady Justices of the Peace for the Borough were sworn in and took their seats on the Bench for the first time on Monday week. (1) Mrs. Manning taking the oath; seated is Miss J. Harrison, LL.D., another of the lady J.P.'s. (2) Signing the declaration. Nearest the camera is Miss Harrison; on her left is Mrs. Bethune Baker, and in the background Mrs. Manning. On the right, leaning over the table, is the Town Clerk (Mr. J. E. L. Whitehead). (3) The lady magistrates hearing their first case. Left to right: Mrs. Bethune Baker, Miss Harrison, Mr. H. E. F. Pateman, the Deputy Mayor (Mr. R. Starr), the Mayor (Mr. G. P. Hawkins), Alderman A. S. Campkin, Mr. W. Few and Mrs. Manning. Underneath, the Deputy Chief Constable (Supt. Hargreaves) and the Magistrates' Clerk, (Mr. Griffith S. Todd).

25

26

27

28

29

31

32

33

34

35

36

37

38

39

40

41

42

43

44

45

46

47

48

49

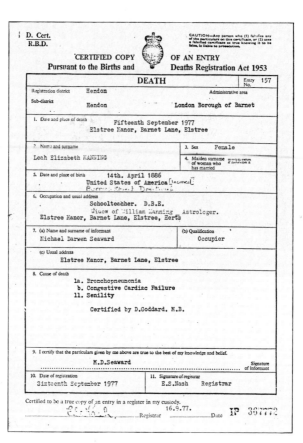

D. Cert.
R.B.D.

CAUTION—Any person who (1) falsifies any of the particulars on this certificate, or (2) uses a falsified certificate as true knowing it to be false, is liable to prosecution.

'CERTIFIED COPY   OF AN ENTRY
Pursuant to the Births and   Deaths Registration Act 1953

DEATH	Entry No. 157

Registration district	Hendon	
Sub-district	Hendon	Administrative area London Borough of Barnet

1. Date and place of death   Fifteenth September 1977
   Elstree Manor, Barnet Lane, Elstree

2. Name and surname   Leah Elizabeth MANNING   3. Sex Female

4. Maiden surname of woman who has married PERRETT

5. Date and place of birth   14th. April 1886
   United States of America [assumed]
   Burren Street Dratford

6. Occupation and usual address   Schoolteacher. D.B.E.
   Widow of William Manning Astrologer.
   Elstree Manor, Barnet Lane, Elstree, Herts

7. (a) Name and surname of informant   (b) Qualification
   Michael Darwen Seaward   Occupier

   (c) Usual address   Elstree Manor, Barnet Lane, Elstree

8. Cause of death
   1a. Bronchopneumonia
   b. Congestive Cardiac Failure
   11. Senility

   Certified by D.Goddard. M.B.

9. I certify that the particulars given by me above are true to the best of my knowledge and belief.
   M.D.Seaward   Signature of informant

10. Date of registration   Sixteenth September 1977   11. Signature of registrar
    E.S.Nash   Registrar

Certified to be a true copy of an entry in a register in my custody.
....Registrar   16.9.77.............Date   IP 367772

50

51

52

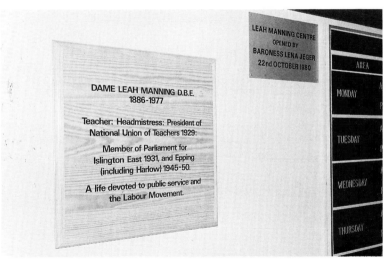

53

54

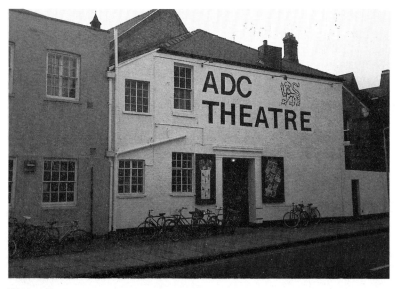

55

commuted to ten years imprisonment. She felt very uncomfortable on this trip and believed she was constantly watched and followed. She recounted this experience at a conference in Bristol on 20th November 1947.

In 1949 she spent a fortnight touring Russian schools and a chorus of disapproval was orchestrated by her opponents in her constituency through the local press. It is interesting that her successor, Graeme Finlay, received no such criticism when he visited Russia. She was badly misrepresented on various issues. These personal and constituency problems, however, paled into insignificance compared to the grave economic, financial and post war reconstruction problems that the Government had had to deal with. In the autumn of 1949, as the Government entered its fifth and final year, there was some expectation of an autumn election and indeed some cabinet members favoured this. Attlee was not convinced and on 13th October said that Parliament would not be dissolved before the end of the year. Prior to the Christmas recess, Herbert Morrison announced that the new session would begin on 24th January 1950, but the historic parliament that dispersed on 16th December 1949 never met again. On 11th January the King agreed to Attlee's wish for a dissolution on February 3rd with the General Election on the 23rd of that month. [Plate 42].

CHAPTER EIGHT
THE 1950 AND 1951 GENERAL ELECTIONS

In Epping constituency three candidates quickly emerged, Leah for Labour, Nigel Davies Conservative, and Peter Lewis for the Liberals. The latter began the campaign by asking the Conservative candidate to stand down as he believed the Liberals could win a straight fight. He feared that unless this could be agreed "the Socialist will retain her seat... I am appealing to you in the national interest." he said. Nigel Davies was not impressed, he told Peter Lewis that no Liberal had been returned for the constituency this century and suggested that in Epping "Liberal Chairmen were as rare as unicorns."

In the first week of the campaign a major political row occurred when the housing committee of Epping Rural District Council refused an application from the Secretary of North Weald Labour Party, a council tenant, to erect a noticeboard in his front garden. The committee had refused the request and decided there should be a prohibition on all front garden noticeboards. In a heated debate it was pointed out that the local constable, also a council tenant, had a large noticeboard in his front garden. In addition, at Netteswell, the Womens Institute, the Football Club and the Parish Council(!), all had noticeboards in front gardens. If one was banned they would all have to be. Mr. Copeland, a labour stalwart from Sheering, put his finger on the real issue, "The reason for this application must be obvious to everyone" he said, "If this board is put up it will be more publicity for Mrs. Manning."

The Council's surveyor, Mr. A.W.R. Webb, pointed out that under the Control of Advertisement Order there was in fact an exemption for boards of less than six square feet advertising local social and other events. For elections there was complete exemption from the Town and Country Planning Acts for any size of advertisement.

The Council resolved to ask the Housing Committee to re-consider its decision!

The West Essex Gazette launched a contest entitled "Everyone is

Guessing" and offered a prize of £5 to the person submitting the nearest forecast of the actual result. A week later it reported that the overwhelming majority were forecasting a Conservative landslide.

Meanwhile Leah had been formally adopted as candidate at a meeting on 31st January, with George A. Smith of Chingford as her Agent. She started her campaign with a meeting at Nazeing on 2nd February chaired by Mr. W.J. Buckley, who told the meeting; "True socialism, as the majority of us know, is not what we have got at the moment. . . this is just a beginning. . . but the Socialist movement intends to go ahead and I aim to have socialism in our time."

Leah said that in spite of all the difficulties the people of the country knew Labour had done a good job. "In four and a half years, we have done more for the people of this country than any Government has done at any time." She pledged that the policy of full employment would be maintained and for the further development of Social Services. Labour, she said, "had given people security and a chance to live." A collection raised 30/- for the election expenses. Later that evening she spoke at Parndon and the following day at High Beach referred to "the one million new homes provided" and pledged "a million more will follow." Her next campaign meeting was at Coopersale and in the following weeks she addressed election rallies at Potter Street, Epping (2), Harlow (2), Waltham Abbey (2), Epping Green, North Weald, Thornwood, Sheering, Upshire, Matching Tye, Roydon, Netteswell and Theydon Bois.

At the Roydon meeting she humoured the audience about her size . . . "If I wasn't the size I am," she said, "I would wear utility." (A range of Government inspired standard clothing and household items produced in the 1940's). The campaign concluded with a rowdy eve of poll meeting in the public hall at Epping which lasted until 11.15 p.m.

Meanwhile,at the Conservative meetings, the threat of the "Red Menace" again emerged. At a meeting at Coopersale, Miss C. Nimmo urged intending Labour voters to consider whether or not they wanted a communist country. What worried her most was that . . . "People would not be free in their own houses."

It was nearly 24 hours after the polls had closed that Labour at the national level was able to claim victory after securing 315 of the 625 parliamentary seats. Despite receiving over a million more votes than in 1945, (13,295,736 to 11,992,292) Labour lost 69 seats - among them Epping, which remained Conservative until 1964. Leah herself had polled 4,000 more votes than in 1945 but was overtaken by Nigel Davies who polled over 9,000 more than the Conservative candidate in 1945. The Liberal lost his deposit. The count, held this time at Chingford, produced the following result:-

Nigel Davies (Con)   24,292
Leah Manning (Lab)   20,385
Peter Lewis (Lib)   4,755
Maj: 3,907

The Gazette "Everyone is guessing" competition was won by Mr. Robert G. Collins of Sumners Farm, Epping Upland, who won £5 with the following forecast:-

Nigel Davies (Con)   24,480
Leah Manning (Lab)   20,549
Peter Lewis   (Lib) 4,681.

Although Labour had retained its Parliamentary majority, the general feeling was that a further election would not be long delayed.

Leah was once again out of the House of Commons. Her personal disappointment was considerable, though she had always recognised her vulnerability, this did not make defeat any sweeter. Personal venom displayed by some of the opposition added to this. For example, two women at the count spat in her face. A leading Labour Party member Joyce Woods demanded an apology from the Tory Party officials present but this was refused. A group at North Weald burnt her effigy outside the Kings Head Inn.

She had come to regard the Epping constituency as her personal responsibility and, indeed, had worked infinitely harder for her constituents than any of her predecessors. Leah always maintained that "legislation is for humanity and the human element must not be lost sight of." The subjects she raised or spoke upon in the Commons reflected her wide interests in parochial, national and international matters but always with a concern for individuals rights and freedoms, see Parliamentary Index (beginning on Page 95).

However her local prestige had been insufficient to counteract the national swing and her rejection, after all her dedicated work, hit her hard. In addition to her political discomfort she needed to find employment to keep going.

Despite losing her seat, Leah remained a popular and powerful figure in local politics. When the Korean war broke out later that year, she supported the action taken by the United Nations which amounted to the despatch of troops by the western allies, led by the United States, to oppose the North Korean advance. She was never a crypto-communist or a fellow-traveller as her enemies tried to depict her. She was most deeply attached to western democracy and western values, although she wanted equally strongly to see international agreement between east and west. On some issues she was not only out of accord with those who sympathised uncritically with the Soviet Union, but also with the Labour left as a whole. She was in some respects inconsistent and she allowed her personal likes or dislikes to take precedence over what might have been a more considered judgement.

This was illustrated in the attitude she adopted towards Sir Stafford Cripps. After his selection at Bristol East in 1929, he was no longer capable of doing right in her eyes. Similarly, when Aneurin Bevan decided to resign in 1951, in protest against the imposition of prescription charges by Hugh Gaitskell, the Labour Chancellor of the Exchequer, after the 1950 General Election, Leah was utterly against him. Despite the fact that Bevan's stand was seen as a revolt against the precedence given to the re-armament programme, which Leah might have been expected to oppose. She roundly denounced him as motivated by ambition, declared her support for Herbert Morrison as successor to Clement Attlee and refused to countenance any word of approval for his actions. She took this stand when the matter was raised at the General Management Committee of the Epping Constituency Labour Party and prevented a motion of support for Bevan being passed, though the increases in prescription charges were denounced.

The expected General Election did not come until the autumn of 1951 when her opponent, in a straight fight, was Graeme B. Finlay, Conservative. Norman Cork, the prospective Liberal candidate, did not contest the election. Labour were hopeful that the replacement of the M.P., Nigel Davies, would benefit them. Leah said that the adoption of Graeme Finlay, who on his own admission "knows nothing about the area" had made Labour "more hopeful of success." He was, she said, "A Scotsman from Wales seeking the votes of an English constituency."

The largest ever adoption meeting – with over 250 members present, was held at Chingford on 5th October and Leah was officially declared the candidate. She said that as a housewife she was pleased "to face the young barrister from Monmouthshire." In 1950 he had opposed Nye Bevan at Ebbw Vale and achieved the distinction of polling the lowest number of votes ever recorded for a Conservative candidate in that constituency. She said there was no sign of him giving up his job as a barrister if he became an M.P., however she thought that "representing this County seat is a full-time job and requires hourly attention."

With her Agent, Alf Brown, they launched the campaign in Epping

Public Hall where a packed and lively meeting listened and heckled both Leah and Hugh Dalton, then Minister of Local Government and Planning. Dalton told the meeting that after six years of Labour rule unemployment was 1% of the insured population - the lowest ever figure in British history. Leah pointed out that in three elections she was now fighting her third male Conservative candidate. "Win or lose, they never stay," she said.

Leah's campaign included meetings at the Meadowview Cafe at Thornwood, Women's Institute Halls at Matching Tye and Netteswell, Village Halls at Roydon, Sheering and Coopersale, school meetings at Upshire, High Beach and Nazeing, in the Queen's Rooms at North Weald, the King's Head Hall Potter Street and eve of poll meetings at Epping, Harlow and Waltham Abbey. Amongst supporting speakers were a host of prominent Labour figures including. Elwyn Jones, Basil Davidson, Francis Noel-Baker, Miss Gladys Sellars, Muriel Nichol, Kingsley Martin, Dorothy Woodman, Haydn Davies, Reg Sorensen and the Earl of Huntingdon.

During the campaign Leah emphasised the need for additional new and replacement schools in the Division. She spoke of the aspirations of working people to be less exploited, have a better standard of living and ensure that their children were well fed and properly educated. She noted with great pleasure how the heights and weights of children had increased in the post war period and the dramatic reduction in the death rate of babies in their first four weeks of life. She found, on doorstep canvassing, that more people were concerned with the issue of war and peace than with the cost of living. In a speech in the Cadet Hut at Nazeing, she said "If we have war this nation comes to an end. The atom bomb bases would be bombed and we could not withstand an atom bomb war." She declared "I desire most passionately to keep the peace of the world and would not call anyone a warmonger."

She admitted to having one day off during the campaign, "I had to pick my crop of Coxs Orange apples before the birds spoilt them." In the event Leah gained 22,598 votes for Labour against 27,392 for the Conservatives, giving Graeme Finlay a majority of 4,794. Labour in fact increased its popular vote to 13,948,385 - with a record 48.77% of those voting. Conservatives and their associates received 13,724,418 votes - 47.98%.

Despite this record of public support the Labour majority of 6 disappeared and a new Conservative administration took office with a 17 seat majority.

Leah, now 65, living at Hatfield Broad Oak, was reported by the Evening Standard as "returning to teaching at 58 after a 21 year break." She gave private tuition at Willow Cottage and also joined the staff of Fedsden, an independent prep school run by her friend Kitty Clare. A few months later, in January 1952, her husband Will died in Addenbrookes Hospital, Cambridge, aged 68.

CHAPTER NINE
THE LATER YEARS

Despite defeat Leah remained active in local politics. At the Epping Constituency Labour Party A.G.M. on 15th January 1955 her Presidential address included the following passage:-

"Through centuries of civilisation man had risen to sublime heights in every department of life and thought and in science and technology he had become a superman. But, as Doctor Schweitzer has pointed out, by some defect of spirit, he had not raised himself to a level of super-human reasoning to correspond to his super human-powers. Schweitzer and Gandhi, two of the greatest men of the age, had in common a quality of compassion. It was their overwhelming love for mankind that separated them out and it was this same attribute which alone could save the world from the dark tragedy that loomed above it. Britain must lead the world in those moral, spiritual and Christian concepts which are also the basis of our Socialist faith."

That same month the new Polling Districts for Harlow had been announced and the first election for the new Urban District Council had been arranged for 26th March. The selection of candidates and their subsequent campaigning raised the political temperature in the town.

On 21st March Leah presided at an election rally at Moot House. She referred to a statement by the Conservative Chairman that the New Towns Act was an agreed measure. Why then, she asked, had the local Tories fought an unprincipled and disgraceful tooth and nail campaign to prevent a new town at Harlow. I say quite explicitly that had I not been Member for the Division at that time - and had we not had a small but resolute Harlow Labour Party in existence, there would have been no Harlow New Town.

1955 was also a year for Essex County Council elections and the question of comprehensive schools became a subject of emotive public debate in the town.

At the Potter Street Labour Party A.G.M. Leah voiced her congratulations to the Branch for urging upon Harlow Labour Party the need for making all local secondary schools comprehensive. This she said was a cardinal point in

Labour's Conference Policy after a most exhaustive enquiry by the Party's educational experts. It would be inexcusable if Labour Essex County Council departed from that policy when they had, in the New Town, an outstanding opportunity of putting it into practice.

In a letter to the Harlow Citizen (1st April 1955) Leah described the eleven plus as:-

"One catastrophic examination taken on one catastrophic day in the life of an immature child. A comprehensive school does not confine itself narrowly to Grammar, Technical and General streams but, by careful cross setting, gives its pupils a chance to develop a rich variety of gifts with which so many of our children are endowed."

In a spirited reply, local teacher, Sheila Hiller, accused local Socialists... "of not understanding the full implications of the term 'comprehensive school'. You do not alter children by pushing them all through the doors of a comprehensive school, as Socialists apparently believe."

However these local issues were overtaken by the news that a General Election would take place on 26th May.

For Leah her last election started with her unanimous adoption at a meeting at the Co-op Hall, Epping on 4th May. Her opponents were Graeme Finlay, the sitting Conservative M.P., and John Arlott, a writer and broadcaster, for the Liberals. Ashley Goff was her agent.

In her adoption speech, Leah criticised the freeze on school buildings, deploring the fact that there were nearly 45,000 classes with more than 40 children. She said "Labour aims at more teachers and better schools and the banishing of the eleven plus examination." She told a later meeting in Harlow that she "would be surprised if there is still an eleven plus examination in the town next year." She spoke of her opposition to the manufacture of the 'H' bomb and described it as "the most frightful menace that has ever faced mankind. Throughout history every weapon of war has been more frightful and more destructive than the last. It had not prevented man from using it. I would not use it and no Christian person would use it. These islands are in mortal danger and nuclear weapons must be banned. Labour in power must begin at once to work on a positive policy for peace."

Leah was strongly supported by local Labour members. Kath White's father, a carpenter, made some steps for Leah to use at open air meetings – they were tested by having three children jump up and down on them. George Thomson (now Lord Thomson of Monifieth), then Labour M.P. for Dundee East, was living in Harlow at the time, but for the last weeks of the campaign he and his wife, Grace, stayed in Dundee. They offered their house to Leah for this period to save the daily journeys to and from Hatfield Broad Oak. The Mark Hall Womens Section formed a support group comprising Mrs. Dixon, Mrs. Druce, Mrs. Kennett, Mrs. Morris and Mrs. Ward. Leah would be given an 8 o'clock morning call – with tea, and whilst she was out campaigning the team looked after the domestic routines of shopping, cleaning and washing – as well as providing a meal when Leah eventually arrived "home".

Labour again conducted a lively campaign which opened on 9th May with meetings at Broadfields School Harlow, Theydon Bois and Roydon. Lord Ogmore, Austin Albu and Reg Sorensen were the supporting speakers. Leah said that Labour would end the feudalism of the tied cottage. She told audiences that a new Labour Government would abolish the eleven plus examination, develop comprehensive schools and have a very big drive to recruit teachers. She said Labour was in favour of the reunification of Germany. On nuclear policy she called for an end to tests and the destruction of stocks. She also called for reductions in armies and air forces and increases in help to under developed countries.

On 18th May she spoke with Elwyn Jones at Victoria Hall and Magdalen Laver Village Hall. Other meetings were held at Epping Upland, Matching, Nazeing, Sheering, Thornwood, North Weald, Chingford, Waltham Abbey, Epping and in Harlow at Churchfield Common Room and Parndon Village Hall. Speakers included the Earl of Listowel, Victor Feather, Lena Jeger and J.P. Brown.

In the 21 day campaign Leah, now 68, addressed 26 indoor meetings and many outdoor gatherings. She gave press conferences and interviews, canvassed and travelled the length and breadth of the huge constituency. Throughout the campaign, John Arlott consistently challenged Graeme Finlay to have a joint meeting of candidates. This was continuously declined. However, one telegram from Arlott surprised the Conservative candidate when the Post Office transmitted "proposed dual meeting" as "proposed duel meeting."

All three candidates were invited to speak at a United Nations Association meeting at Moot House on 21st May chaired by Gerald Palmer, a local headmaster. John Arlott, the Liberal candidate, appeared but Graeme Finlay declined the invitation. In a discussion on House of Commons voting Leah said she had when necessary – such as on the extension of National Service, voted against the party line. "The whips cannot control my conscience" she said.

It was a brave campaign and, as the West Essex Gazette forecast, the result would depend on the Liberal performance. The Harlow Citizen forecast a Conservative victory. In the event John Arlott saved his deposit with 7,528 votes. Both the Conservative and Labour votes fell from 1951 when it had been a straight fight. Leah gained 22,542 – just 56 short of her 1951 total, whilst Graeme Finlay lost 1,327 votes to reach 26,065 and to win the seat on a reduced majority of 3,523. Leah had always hoped that the increase in voters in the New Town would swing the constituency back into the Labour camp but this did not occur. As she reflected on her third successive defeat she sadly decided that it was time for her to retire from the Parliamentary stakes. She announced her decision at a Constituency dinner on the 16th June.

At the meeting of the Constituency Party General Management Committee on the 18th June the following resolution was adopted:-

"This meeting of Epping Constituency Labour Party accepts with the deepest regret the decision of Mrs. Leah Manning not to contest the Division again. It places on record its gratitude for the magnificent service which Mrs. Manning has rendered the Party and the Constituency since 1945 and in recognition of those services invites her to become Life President of the Constituency Labour Party so that her experience and inspiration may continue to be available to the Party."

Commenting upon her withdrawal, the editorial of the Harlow Citizen stated:-

"Mrs. Manning had been a worthy champion of Labour's cause in the area, and, apart from her political activities she will be remembered as a good M.P. and candidate as her 'case-book' work has been a notable feature of her activities."

Clement Attlee and his wife came to her retirement party [Plate 43] and the former made a touching speech. The Harlow Citizen on 7th October 1955 carried a front page picture of the Attlees at the event. The paper's editorial said that no report of the occasion could be given as the paper had not been invited. It had been given a hand-out but its absence from the event prevented it from printing an unbiased report. The editorial concluded:-

"The "Harlow Citizen" in common with all freedom- loving newspapers, will resist this tendency to the end."

Many of her supporters were deeply saddened by her departure, though they recognised it had to come. However, she kept in touch with Labour Party affairs and continued her long association with the Women's Section at Chingford.

Once again she returned to teaching at Fedsden. She worked three hours a day for five days – teaching English, Biology and History – including

Constitutional History. The school had started at Roydon and due to expansion, took over Parndon Hall, Harlow and used Kingsmoor House for the boarders.

It was arranged that Sam Robinson, one of Kitty's assistants would collect Leah from Willow Cottage in the school bus. This had a very high tailboard and Sam always took along a box to form a step for Leah to get on board. Unfortunately when Sam was away his deputy, Peter Cope, arrived without the box. After some consideration of the problem, it was decided that Leah would put one foot up and Peter would give her a bunk-up the rest of the way with his shoulder! With some amusement she was eventually safe on board.

Later, when it was decided to apply for recognition by the then Department of Education and Science, it was necessary to divide the juniors and seniors, the former staying at Parndon Hall and the stables and the seniors moving to Kingsmoor House. The Inspector's report, recommending recognition, included the following reference to Leah:-

"It is here (in the top class) that the work in History comes to life in the lessons taken by an elderly but gifted and vigorous teacher." During one festive season Leah took the senior girls to the local church to prepare for the annual carol concert. Kitty's husband, Leonard, was acting as pianist. Leah was a hard taskmaster and during a long and tiring rehearsal she berated everyone present for lack of effort and harmony. At the conclusion as they came away Leonard smiled wryly and confided in Kitty:-"Another session like that and we'll have to think about reconsecrating the church to Leah." Former staff and pupils of Fedsden have an annual re-union in Harlow and memories of Leah are always recalled with affection, humour and gratitude.

Kitty and Leah eventually changed Kingsmoor House into a mother and baby home where unmarried mothers could live and work. In January 1974 the empty house was bought by Harlow Council and after renovation and restoration, opened as a Family Centre.

In the autumn of the following year the Anglo French attack on Egypt provoked nationwide protest. In Harlow open air meetings were held outside Moot House (9th November 1956) and in the Market Square. At the latter meeting a lone Tory parked her car and held her hand on the hooter trying to drown out what Leah was saying. However, with the microphone on top of a cafe roof, she was more than a match for the interruption which was ignored.

Speakers expressed their concern at the shame and humiliation of the country by Eden's actions. A telegram was sent to the Government urging that all hostilities should cease at once, that all troops be recalled and that the U.N.Charter should not be contravened again.

The following week Leah spoke at a meeting at St. Andrew's Methodist Church at which the Minister, the Reverend Eryl Hughes and other clergy defended the protest they had made. Len White, a prominent community figure, said:-"Judged by Christian standards of behaviour I find it extremely difficult to support the bombing of a smaller nation to maintain our standard of living." A collection of £7 was sent to Egypt for war relief work. Harlow Council sent a strongly worded telegram to the Government urging compliance with United Nations policies and principles.

At the end of 1956, Leah left teaching to become Personnel Manager and a Director of J & B. Cabinets in Harlow. She set up a consultative committee, provided a decent canteen and set up a Women's Department on semi-skilled work. However, for various reasons, the following year she returned to her first love - teaching. She continued to be active both in local politics - speaking at public meetings and in the press on local and national issues. She was furthermore continually approached to assist with personal problems and made her contribution in the locality in many other ways.

When the Epping Constituency Labour Party looked for a successor, Leah supported Shirley Williams, the daughter of her former running mate at Sunderland, George Catlin, and his wife Vera Brittain. A second group promoted Peter Shore but the Constituency Party, perhaps as a compromise, selected Donald Ford [Plate 44] and the other candidates went elsewhere.

The result of the 1959 General Election in the Epping Constituency was:-

Graeme Finlay (Con)	31507
Donald Ford (Lab)	27114
John Arlott (Lib)	11913

Leah Manning continued to attend both N.U.T. and Labour Party Conferences but she was unhappy about some of the developments in Labour circles. Despite her initial reaction to Aneurin Bevan's resignation in 1951, she did not approve of Hugh Gaitskell's opposition to the left and to C.N.D. She did not even approve of him when he offended most of his friends on the right at the 1962 Labour Party Conference by his passionate declaration of opposition to Britain's entry into the E.E.C. Leah had joined the Federal Union in the 1940's. She deeply sympathised with the objective of European Unity. She found his stand on this issue totally out of accord with her views.

Leah always retained the strong affinity with Christian Socialism that she had developed from her friendship with Stewart Headlam. In 1945 she was closely involved in the preparation of the Christian Socialist Manifesto entitled "In This Faith We Live."

Soon after the 1945 election, a Parliamentary Christian Socialist Group was formed under the Chairmanship of Tom Skeffington-Lodge (Labour M.P. for Bedford). Leah became an active member of the Group which had nearly one hundred members mostly in the Commons – but a few in the Lords. It held fringe meetings at Labour Party Annual Conferences.

In the early 1960's Leah was involved in the formation of a Mid-Essex Branch – this comprised of members from three towns, four villages and Harlow New Town. As the latter grew, it became a separate branch with Mary and Bob Guy, Jim Desormeaux and Clarice Mort among its active nucleus. Leah ruefully recalled one weekend event organised at the invitation of Father Wainwright, in the Vicarage Garden of St. Mary Magdalene at Potter Street. It poured with rain, the speaker failed to arrive – as did the coach party from London. After tea the rain cleared and a lovely English summer evening developed and everyone walked across the common to church for Evensong. It was, she said, "A beautiful stroll in the cool of the evening countryside."

Leah and Ruth Dalton, wife of her old friend Hugh had opened the first Family Planning Clinic in Cambridge around 1920. She maintained a lifelong interest and involvement in the F.P.A. Over 40 years later she was the driving force in establishing the first clinic in Harlow at Nuffield House. Others involved included Elizabeth Hills as Senior Doctor with John Druce as Treasurer and Elvira Druce as Clinics Organiser – Leah frequently acted as Chairman and Secretary. The first five clients soon became thousands and the clinic quickly expanded from one to seven nights a week. Later Leah became President of the Herts and Beds Branch of the Association.

At the 1964 National Annual General Meeting at Church House Westminster, Leah proposed a motion that Clinics should give contraceptive advice to unmarried women. Seconding the proposal Mrs. Ponsonby said:-

"the new pattern of (pre-marital) sexual behaviour had come to stay and that approval or disapproval should play no part in the Association's attitude."

The motion was heavily defeated by an amendment stating that unmarried people seeking clinic advice should be referred to the Youth Advisory Centres. The national policy did not deter the establishment of a local advisory group – assisted by Dr. Bach and a range of local professionals and volunteers who supported the idea. Although they were disappointed by the conference decision the publicity it caused actually assisted the project in

Harlow. Leah was asked to write two articles for the News of the World and the fees received enabled her, with Pamela Heeks and others, to progress the setting up of an advisory clinic. Grants were obtained from Harlow Development Corporation and Harlow Council. After many refusals of accommodation, the clinic met initially at a Community Centre - Northbrooks House, Harlow. A year later it was able to move into a local Health Centre at Chadwick House.

In the 1966 Honours List Leah was made a Dame Commander of the Order of the British Empire, for political and public services. Kitty Clare drove Leah to Buckingham Palace for investiture by the Queen.

In 1970 Leah published her autobiography "A Life For Education" which covered her experiences over more than 80 years.

In reviewing the book, Tom Skeffington-Lodge wrote:-

"From an early age she felt that her Christian beliefs could best be expressed in a practical way through membership of the Labour Party. Throughout her life she sought to insist that it should base its policies on a clear moral purpose designed to bring about human betterment at home and abroad."

At the 1970 N.U.T. Conference, Leah presented a cheque for £250 to the Benevolent Fund - this represented the entire estimated royalties from the 4,500 run. At the end of the Conference she raced back home to see her beloved cat, Che Guevara, which had been detained at the local vet with a serious infection.

She also maintained many of her old friendships outside the area. She never ceased to admire Barbara Castle and dedicated her autobiography to her. Barbara visited her at her home at Willow Cottage. On the other hand she would have Sarah Barker, the most redoubtable pillar of Labour Party orthodoxy, to stay with her. It was Sarah Barker who warned her against a nefarious left winger, Stan Newens, who was seeking to obtain the nomination as the prospective Labour Parliamentary candidate in her old constituency. This did not stop Leah Manning, who had herself uttered harsh words against this aspirant to the House of Commons, from writing a glowing reference to assist him in persuading the National Executive Committee to endorse his candidature. She spoke for him in Harlow in the 1964, 1966 and 1970 General Election campaigns and would still have been willing to take on certain public offices at that time. Indeed in 1974 she was a member of a Government panel studying sex education.

Leah Manning lived out her retirement as long as she could at Willow Cottage [Plates 45–47] - a delightful thatched residence in the pretty Essex village of Hatfield Broad Oak- just outside the boundaries of Epping Constituency. Always a Christian as well as a Socialist, she took an increasing interest in the Parish Church of St. Mary the Virgin [Plate 48]. As the years passed and when it was no longer possible to take Communion there, she arranged for the Vicar to call to administer the sacrament in her own home. She continued to drive until she was eighty years of age and she was still teaching with Kitty Clare at eighty four. As her health deteriorated, she found travelling more and more difficult.

In her last years at Willow Cottage she was regularly visited by Jeanne Pugh of Harlow and lovingly cared for by her housekeeper - Mrs. Joan Ingold.

Eventually, however, she agreed to leave Hatfield Broad Oak and for a while was accommodated with Dr. Ross until she went to Elstree Manor, the N.U.T. Home for Retired Teachers. [Plate 49]. She died there on 15th September 1977. [Plate 50] Her husband, with whom she ceased to live on a regular basis many years previously, had died in 1952. As there were no surviving children of the marriage, she had no direct descendants and her will provided that after a £4000 bequest to Joan Ingold, the remainder of £17310 should go towards the building of a hall for Hatfield Broad Oak Church. The Parochial Church Council are hoping that this wish will eventually be fulfilled. It is also intended to place in the church a commemorative plaque to Leah.

Most of her brothers and sisters pre-deceased her, but one sister, Mrs. Dorothy Edwards, was still alive at Wichita, Kansas, U.S.A. in 1980. On the other hand numerous nieces, nephews, and their descendants still live and flourish in Canada and the U.S.A. and cherish her memory.

Leah donated her body for medical research and there was no funeral. A memorial service was, however, organised at Hatfield Broad Oak church on Sunday 6th November 1977. The Reverend J. Beresford Weller officiated and there were tributes from Mrs. Lena Jeger M.P. on behalf of the National Executive Committee of the Labour Party and from Mr.A.J.Wilshire, a former President of the National Union of Teachers. The Reverend A.D. Jones, the former Vicar, gave an address and Stan Newens M.P. read the lesson. The Church was packed.

Nearly three years later on 20th October 1980, Baroness Jeger (formerly Lena Jeger M.P.) visited Harlow to unveil a commemorative plaque at a new Social and Recreational Centre,built by Harlow Council for retired people, and formally named the Leah Manning Centre. [Plates 51-53] The audience included many who had worked with her and who had striven to achieve some permanent memorial to her in the town. Among these were Councillor Rene Morris, Ron and Kath White, Sir Frederick and Lady Gibberd, Ted Woodland, Elvira and John Druce and Kitty Clare. The Chairman of Council, Roy Collyer, welcomed guests and Stan Newens M.P. also spoke.

Leah Manning was an outstanding person who achieved great distinction despite the obstacles which barred the progress of women in public life in her early years. She was a pioneer of many of the objectives which were realised in her lifetime and which today are taken for granted.

She was a powerful personality and it was inevitable that she clashed with those who stood in the way of the things she was aiming to bring about. She could be domineering and intolerant. She would seek to determine the conduct and decisions of a meeting whether she was in the Chair herself or elsewhere on the platform.

Her ideas furthermore were not always acceptable, even among those who stood closest to her. Despite her immense contribution to educational advance, she was unconvinced on some aspects of the policies adopted by the National Association of Labour Teachers, which she helped to found. At one time she was not prepared to accept that comprehensive schools should provide for all pupils at the secondary stage, but subsequently became a firm advocate.

Overall, however, she was a woman of immense compassion and drive with a vision of a better society which inspired her throughout her life. Furthermore, her sights were not limited to Britain, deeply as she loved her native land. She travelled extensively in Europe including visits to France, Germany, Holland, Poland, Rumania, Russia, Spain, Switzerland and Yugoslavia and went to Canada for two holidays and to America a number of times for lecture tours and family visits. She worked in the Federal Union for a United Europe. She was profoundly concerned about the rights and living standards of people throughout the world. She reacted angrily against Fascism, racism and discrimination in any form. She was possessed of a vast fund of experience, built up over the years in many different environments, and this gave her a great breadth of vision and power of understanding. Yet in the last analysis she retained the basis of the Christian faith which she received from her family – this was really the basis of her philosophy of life.

Leah remained a staunch individualist throughout her life. She enjoyed the "great good fortune of a wide circle of affectionate friends." She wrote in her autobiography "We come into the world alone we must leave it alone. One can come to terms with the world and come to terms with oneself, but one must leave a solitude within the heart. Only thus can one consciously listen to the voice within; the voice which gives certainty and coherence to life and the universe." Leah loved England and the English countryside and was never happier than when she could retreat to her thatched cottage at Hatfield Broad Oak.

She was always a strong campaigner for the preservation and protection of the Essex countryside and had a particular affection for Waltham Abbey – part of her constituency. She was never short of humour – particularly about her size. She enjoyed visiting the cinema, and was a life-long theatregoer, and for some years a Director of Unity Theatre. [Plate 54]. She liked amateur dramatics and in her Cambridge days she frequently played the lead in productions at the A.D.C. Theatre in Green Street. [Plate 55]. During those years she also enjoyed choral singing with the University Musical Society. Throughout her life, she was an avid reader and by the age of ten had read Scott and Dickens. She was equally at home with the classics or thriller fiction. She loved the poetry of Browning, Gerald Manley Hopkins, Keats, Swinburne and the Shakespeare Sonnets. Indeed she confessed that her love for literature, poetry and classical music were the formative influences on her outlook.

Her life contained many notable journeys – perhaps in her reflective moments she silently spoke a verse of a poem she knew, The English Roads, by Gideon Clark.

> *The plain white roads of England*
> *With elm and hazel lined,*
> *When hard fate holds me from them*
> *I tread them in my mind.*

Leah was, of course, a product of all those influences which helped her to make a contribution of unique value to the local and wider community in which she spent her distinguished life.

BIBLIOGRAPHY

A Life For Education, Leah Manning, Victor Gollanz, 1970.

What I Saw In Spain, Leah Manning, Victor Gollanz, 1935.

Growing Up - Labour's Plan for Women and Children, Leah Manning, Labour Party, 1948.

The Signal That Was Spain (The Aid to Spain Movement in Britain 1936-1939), Jim Fyrth, Lawrence & Wishart, 1986.

Searchlight on Spain, Katherine Marjory, Penguin, 1938.

Red Roses for Isobel. (The life of Isobel Brown), May Hill, Preston Community Press, 1982.

Stewart Headlam, E.G. Bettany, John Murray, 1926.

Centenary History of the London County Council, Hambledon Press.

Hugh Dalton, Memoirs in Three Volumes, Hugh Dalton, Frederick Müller, 1953-1962.

Herbert Morrison. Portrait of a Politician, Bernard Donoughue and G.W. Jones, Weidenfeld & Nicholson, 1973.

Women At Westminster, Pamela Brookes, Peter Davies, 1967.

Labour and the Left in the 1930's, Ben Pimlott, Cambridge University Press, 1977.

Labour in Power, 1945-1951, Kenneth O. Morgan, Oxford University Press, 1984.

The Vote, Journal of the Womens Freedom League.

Dictionary of Labour Biography (pp. 166-172), MacMillan, 1984.

Labour Party Journals.

The Schoolmaster and Woman Teachers Chronicle. (and other Journals), National Union of Teachers.

East London Record, East London History Society.

Cambridge Labour Party - Silver Jubilee Booklet, Cambridge Labour Party.

Hansard.

The Times (and Indices).

West Essex Gazette.

Harlow Citizen.

Cambridge Daily News.

Sunderland Echo.

For other sources please refer to the Acknowledgements.

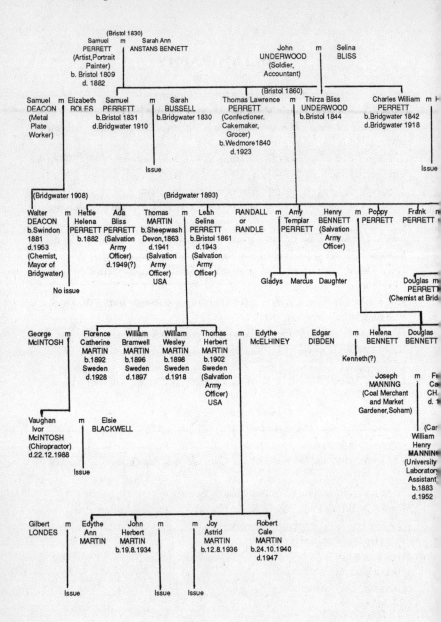

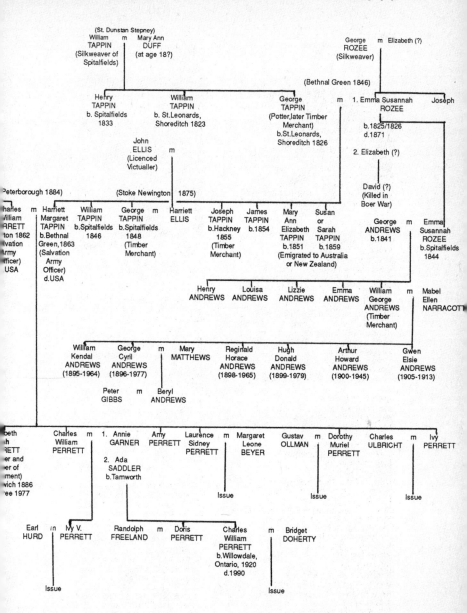

MANNING/PERRETT FAMILY TREE

INDEX

PARLIAMENTARY INDEX

(Subjects that Leah raised or spoke upon during her Parliamentary career. Further information on these subjects can be found by reference to the appropriate Hansard indices for the years 1931 and 1945/50.)

- Opthalmic Services
- Opticians
- Parkinsons Disease
- Plastic Dentures
- Teachers Medicals
National Institute of Houseworkers
National Insurance - Child Benefits
- Student Credits
National Insurance Bill
National Mark Scheme
National Parks and Access to the Countryside Bill
National Service - Amendment Bill
- Bill
Navy - Officers
- Vaccination
Nazeing - Bus Services
- Flooding
- School Sanitation
Netteswell Church School
New Town
New Towns - Bill
- Building Licences
Nigeria, Teachers Salaries
North Atlantic Treaty
Nurseries and Childminders Bill
Nurses
Nurses Bill
Nyasaland Prisoners

Old Age Pensions
Ordnance Factories
Overseas Resources Development Bill
Overseas Visitors.

Palestine
Paraffin
Parliament Bill
Pensions and Grants
Pershore Camp
Personal - Explanation
- Statement
Persons Guilty of Murder
Petrol - Abolition Order
- Allowances
- Basic Ration
- Commercial Travellers
- Motor Coaches
- S. & E. Coupons
- Smallholders
- Supplementary Coupons
- Unused Rations of
Pharmaceutical Preparations
Points of Order
Poland - British Industries
- M. Mikolajczyk
- Relations with
- Resettlement Bill

- Resettlement Corps.
- Situation
- Trade Negotiations
Poles - Deportation
- Re M. Zaleski
Police Traffic Control
Police Women
Polish Resettlement Bill
Political Propaganda
Post Office Telephones
Potato Rationing
Prisoners Letters
Prisoners of War - Cashing of Credits
- Coupons
- Employment
- Marriage
Probation of Offenders Bill
Productivity
Peterlin Professor, Detention
Purchase Tax

Queue Priority, Mothers

Railways - Central Line
- School Journeys
- Station Slot Machines
Refrigerator Ships
Representation of the People Bill
River Boards Bill
Road Transport Fares
Roydon - Mr. R.E. Jeffrey
- Rail Services
Russian Womens Visit

Scientific Biologists
Scientific Research
Shipping of Wild Animals
Shrewsbury - Mr.J. Green
Signposting of Footpaths
Silverthorne Telephone Exchange
Sittings of the House - Hours
Slot Machines
Smoke Abatement
Soap Ration
Sound Films
South Tyrol
Spain
Spain - Diplomatic Relations
- Franco Regime
- National Prisoners
Spanish Nationals
Speed Limits
Sterling Exchange Rate
Suburban Rail Services
Sudan, Female Circumcision
Suits, Purchase Tax
Supplies and Services Bill